BECOMING A WEB HOSTING PROVIDER

ACHIEVING AMBITIONS: AN ENTREPRENEUR'S JOURNEY TO DIGITAL SUCCESS

DEPREDURAND NICOLAS

BECOMING A WEB HOSTING PROVIDER !

Nicolas Depredurand

Nicolas Depredurand, Becoming a Web Hosting Provider!
Self-publishing - Copyright © 2024

❀ Created with Vellum

DEDICATION

To the one who shares my life, the mother of my children, This book, a reflection of an extraordinary journey, is the result of a path I could never have undertaken without your love, unwavering support, and belief in my dreams. You have been my beacon in the darkness, my refuge in the storm, and the constant source of my inspiration. Through every page, I weave not only my story but also the lessons you have taught me: strength, compassion, and the importance of dedication. This book is an ode to the power you have given me, the happiness you have brought into my life, and the spirit of entrepreneurship you have always encouraged. With all my gratitude and deep love, Nicolas

NOTE TO READERS

In the context of this work, I mention various companies, some of which still exist in their current form, others having evolved or ceased their activities. It is important to emphasize that these references are based on my personal perspective and observations at the time they are mentioned in the text. My intention is in no way to harm the reputation or image of these companies. These mentions are made for informational or illustrative purposes and reflect only my point of view, without claiming to be a comprehensive or updated analysis of the situation of these entities. I fully recognize that the business and organizational landscape is dynamic and subject to change, and consequently, my comments are based on information available and interpreted at a given time.

Furthermore, a glossary is included at the end of the book to enhance your understanding of the technical and specialized terms used throughout this book.

BECOMING A WEB HOSTING PROVIDER !

Nicolas Depredurand

FIRST STEPS: BETWEEN SELF-TAUGHT LEARNING AND PERSEVERANCE

My foray into the world of web hosting began in quite a unique way: a remote internship, a practice not common in 1998. This internship challenged me to become self-taught, forcing me to learn on my own in a still nascent digital world. Armed with a 14k modem, patience was my virtue; every page loaded, every bit of information gleaned, was a victory in itself.

At that time, resources for learning were scarce, especially in Épinal where I lived. Books and guides on programming and web design were precious commodities, hard to find. Fortunately, occasional trips to Paris with my father opened a window to a world of knowledge for me. The Virgin Megastore on the Champs-Élysées became my Aladdin's cave, where I could find all the books and resources I needed to quench my thirst for learning.

Each trip to Paris was also an opportunity to visit the famous Montgallet street, known for its computer stores.

There, I gathered parts to assemble PCs that I would then sell back in Épinal. This activity was more than a hobby; it was a way to increase my resources to fund my individual business project. Each PC sold brought me a little closer to my dream. This period was marked by an entrepreneurial spirit and a desire for autonomy. Working remotely, learning as a self-taught individual, assembling and selling PCs: each step was a learning experience, each challenge overcome shaped me as an entrepreneur. It was in this environment that I laid the first stones of what would become LWS.

Bold Beginnings and Self-Directed Learning

My entrepreneurial journey began in a unique context. While concurrently pursuing my studies in industrial computer science, I ventured into the world of the web, not as a freelancer – a concept not widely recognized at the time – but as an individual entrepreneur. This era was for me a time of discovery and active exploration of the infinite potential of the Internet.

School: A Contrast to My Aspirations and a Revealing Anecdote

During my studies in industrial computer science, I felt a stark contrast between the academic program and my personal aspirations. Courses focused on C coding and the use of software like Word and Excel bored me, seeming disconnected from the ongoing digital revolution.

Vindication through Results: Triumph in the Oral Exam

My experience in the business management course, which included analyzing financial statements, took an unexpected and revealing turn. I was excluded from the course after only a month, due to a divergence of perspectives with the professor, but I approached the final exam with renewed determination. This entirely oral exam was my chance to prove my ability to succeed outside traditional teaching methods.

Discovery of a Hidden Talent : Communication and Persuasion

At the exam, I surprised not only the examiners but also myself. Despite missing the classes, I scored 19/20, the highest mark of my class. More than a mere academic success, this event was a defining moment where I discovered my natural talent for communication. When I talk about topics I'm passionate about, my ability to captivate the audience and pique their interest becomes evident. This ease of expressing my ideas, clearly articulating my thoughts, and convincing with passion turned out to be a valuable asset in my entrepreneurial journey.

Leveraging this Talent in My Entrepreneurship

This ability to communicate effectively became a cornerstone of my professional success. It allowed me to share my vision with clarity and conviction, to rally people to my ideas, and to navigate successfully in the business world. This talent, revealed in an unexpected academic context, played a crucial role in the founding and development of my business, enabling me to convince clients, partners, and investors of the value and innovation of my projects.

Entrepreneurialism and Self-Education

Determined to forge my own path, I delved into creating websites. This period was marked by intense self-taught learning. I immersed myself in studying PHP and MySQL, as well as graphic design through Photoshop. These self-taught skills were crucial for providing comprehensive and quality web services.

Funding the Dream : Working to Innovate

To fund my ambitions, I took up a position at the Michelin factory in Golbey, adopting a five-eight work shift pattern. This intense work allowed me to build the capital necessary to rent my first server – a crucial step towards realizing my dream. This server would host my own websites as well as those of my future clients.

LWS: From Idea to Reality

All these efforts, this thirst for learning, and this hard work were the foundations of LWS. Each challenge I overcame, each piece of knowledge I acquired, each PC I assembled and sold brought me closer to realizing my project. It was not just the beginning of a company; it was the birth of a vision to offer quality web hosting accessible to everyone.

LWS: An Unexpected and Creative Birth

The genesis of LWS is the result of unexpected circumstances and my penchant for creation. Originally, my primary interest lay in web design, a field where I could express my creativity. Web hosting was for me a practical necessity rather than a passion. However, with an increasing number of sites to host, the need to find an adequate hosting solution became more pressing.

A Decisive Turn: An Inspiring Advertisement from Skyturn

The trigger for my foray into the world of web hosting was an advertisement noticed in a computer magazine, signed by Skyturn. This company, endowed with significant capital and avant-garde in Europe, had, unknowingly, invented the concept of VPS (Virtual Private Server).

Their slogan, "Become a web host," was not just a catchphrase; it was a promise of technological innovation.

The All-in-One Server Revelation

What truly captured my attention was the promise of a hosting solution without technical constraints, which seemed perfectly suited to my needs. Skyturn's offer included a server equipped with APACHE, MYSQL, MAIL, FTP, DNS - in short, everything needed to efficiently host websites. The most revolutionary aspect was the intuitive web interface, allowing easy management of sites, emails, DNS, and more. Everything was interfaced, a remarkable innovation for the time.

The Innovation of 1998-99: A Pioneering Concept

In 1998-99, such an offer was unheard of. It represented a major advance in the field of web hosting, and I was fascinated by this technology. I would have loved to have been the originator of such innovation. Naively, I saw in this solution the ideal answer to my needs: it allowed me to focus on creating websites while providing a reliable and easy-to-manage hosting service for my own creations and those of my clients.

A Revolutionary Interface: Precursor to Modern VPS

Skyturn's Antologic offer was ahead of its time, foreshadowing what we know today as VPS (Virtual Private Server). It provided me with a server that, while conceptually similar to today's VPS, was a real innovation twenty years ago. The interface offered by Skyturn was truly revolutionary. Simple and intuitive, it allowed the installation and configuration of websites, email accounts, FTP servers, and much more, all in just a few minutes. This ease of use was unprecedented at the time.

Economical and Managed : An All-in-One Solution

In addition to its ease of use, this solution offered a significant economic advantage over a dedicated server. It was also managed, meaning that Skyturn took care of the maintenance and updates, thus freeing me from these technical constraints. This outsourced management was a major asset, allowing me to fully dedicate myself to my passion for web development and creation.

Focus on Creation and Development

Thanks to this solution, I could focus on what I loved most: developing in PHP/MYSQL, creating with Photoshop, and building in HTML. This freedom to concentrate on creation and development without worrying about the technical aspects of hosting was a key factor in my professional growth and the initial success of Ligne Web Services, which would become LWS.

Details: At the time, many sites were developed with Microsoft FrontPage. This software was particularly favored for its simplicity in adding visitor counters and forms, which were in high demand. However, for these elements to function properly, a compatible server was required. Skyturn had managed to integrate these functionalities, especially for counters and certain other FrontPage-specific features. This allowed me to easily meet a wide range of requests, which was essential at that time. In contrast, Linux servers offering pseudo compatibility with ASP and FrontPage, such as Cobalt servers, were expensive, had poor ASP and FrontPage performance, and were less accessible to many users.

Creation of Ligne Web and Evolution to LWS

The Launch of Ligne Web: A Concrete Commitment. The discovery of Skyturn's offer was the catalyst for the creation of my company, Ligne Web. It was the official start of my foray into the world of web hosting. This step marked the union of my passion for website creation with the practical needs of hosting them, a balance between creativity and functionality.

First Supplier Contract: A Significant Commitment

The opening of Ligne Web was accompanied by a decisive moment: the signing of my first supplier contract with Skyturn for hosting. This contract was not just a simple administrative formality; it represented a real and serious commitment. For me, it was a crucial step that meant there was no turning back. This decision committed all my savings, symbolizing my total investment in this project. It was a bet on the future, driven by the conviction that my business could succeed.

Transition to LWS and Simplification of the Name

Over time and as the business evolved, the transition to a SARL (limited liability company) structure became necessary (I will come back to this a few years later). This change required simplifying the company's name. My accountant at the time played a key role in this process by suggesting shortening Ligne Web to LWS. Thus, Ligne Web Services was born. This change, born of chance and the quest for simplicity, marked a new stage in the company's development, making it more identifiable and accessible.

Context of the Time: During this period, I was still living at my parents' house in a small village near Épinal. We did not have access to ADSL, and my parents did not have the financial means to provide substantial support in this area. The only help I requested and received was the installation of a Numéris line from France Télécom. Going from a 14Kbit/s to 128Kbit/s connection was a real revolution for me. Although it may seem insignificant today, at the time, the difference was huge and meaningful. This improvement in internet connectivity, although quite costly for my parents, was a key element in my ability to move forward with my project.

My First Website and Acquiring the First Customers

With Ligne Web now operational, it was time to embark on the quest for clients. The first crucial step was the creation of my own website to promote and sell my services. This site was not just a showcase of my web design skills but also an essential commercial tool for offering web hosting.

Technical Challenges: Domain Search Module and Credit Card Payments

One of the biggest challenges was developing a module for searching the availability of domain names. At that time, such a tool was complex to design and integrate. Similarly, implementing a credit card payment system was a daunting task. Selling web design services was relatively straightforward – often, an online form was sufficient. However, combining the sale of web hosting and managing automated payments was another matter entirely.

Hours of Work for a Successful First Version

I invested many hours to overcome these technical challenges. It was necessary to ensure not only the functionality of the site but also a smooth and secure user experience. Despite the hurdles, I managed to launch the first version of the site. This launch marked a turning point: I could now offer a complete and automated web hosting service, a significant asset at a time when this convenience was not yet commonplace.

Attracting the First Customers: A Turn Towards Web Hosting

Initially, seeking clients for web design proved more complex than anticipated. This activity required considerable time, especially since I had to juggle it with my studies. Paradoxically, clients looking for web hosting services began to flow in naturally. This growing demand gradually steered me towards specializing in web hosting.

Specializing in Hosting: Responding to Market Demand

Unlike web design, web hosting quickly emerged as a field in high demand.

I noticed that many clients were primarily interested in reliable and affordable hosting solutions. This trend led me to focus more on this segment, which involved managing customer support, creating documentation, troubleshooting for clients, and constantly improving site features like order and payment forms.

Expanding the Business and Making the Server Profitable

This specialization required a lot of time and effort but proved to be the most promising path for the development of my business. Managing web hosting was both demanding and rewarding. To make the server profitable and ensure the growth of the business, I needed to attract more clients. Each new web hosting subscription was another step towards solidifying my business and affirming my presence in the hosting market.

Strategic Transition: The Discontinuation of Ligne Web

Following the success of A-a-hebergement.com and its effectiveness in quickly attracting a larger clientele, I made the strategic decision to completely detach from the Ligne Web site.

This decision was not trivial: it marked a significant evolution in my commercial and strategic approach. Ligne Web, while being the starting point of my adventure in web hosting, no longer corresponded to the direction I wanted to take nor to the market requirements as dictated by platforms like Yahoo.

Focusing Resources on a Winning Strategy

This transition allowed me to concentrate all my resources and energy on A-a-hebergement.com. By focusing on a single site that had proven itself in terms of visibility and the ability to generate client traffic, I was able to optimize my efforts and refine my service offering.

The discontinuation of Ligne Web was a crucial step in streamlining my activity, allowing me to fully commit to a strategy that had clearly shown its effectiveness.

A Future-Oriented Decision

This decision to discontinue Ligne Web reflected my commitment to following market trends and adapting my business to the changing realities of the web hosting world. It also symbolized a willingness to grow and evolve, proving my ability to make bold decisions for the success of my business.

Details: Today, many wonder why I manage multiple sites, including A-a-hebergement.com and seven others. The answer is rooted in experiences such as that of Ligne Web. These different sites were the result of continuous testing and experimentation in the field of online sales. My strategy was simple: choose a name beginning with an 'A' for better visibility in rankings, and then develop a site around that name. If a site performed better than Ligne Web, I focused on it. This approach allowed me to test various methods to stand out, generate revenue, and evolve in the industry. My investment in terms of time was huge, but I was driven by natural curiosity and a wealth of ideas. Each site was a new adventure, a new opportunity to learn and grow in the profession. Was this strategy, creating several sites rather than focusing on a single brand, the best solution? In hindsight, I'm not sure. At the time, I lacked the financial means to promote a brand that wasn't well-ranked in search engines. I did not want to borrow or seek investors. I favored independence and the possibility of growing at my own pace, even if it meant exploring several paths simultaneously. I will detail this viewpoint on investment and borrowing later.

The Decision to Go It Alone: Between Apprehensions and Convictions

At the very beginning, the idea of embarking on an entrepreneurial adventure alone was somewhat intimidating to me.

I had considered partnering with others, but these attempts did not come to fruition for various reasons. Some did not believe in me or in my project, others were afraid to take the leap. Despite these rejections, my determination to create my own company remained unshakable. For me, the idea of not getting started was simply inconceivable.

Refusal of a Conventional Career Path

I knew that a traditional job would never allow me to realize the dreams I had in mind. The world of conventional work seemed too restrictive, too far removed from what I wanted to achieve.

I was looking for a field where I could experiment, tinker, explore new technologies, and navigate the internet, my favorite playground. At that time, the digital landscape was already fascinating, and I'm not even talking about advances like YouTube or artificial intelligence that have become pillars of the modern web.

A Vision Driven by Passion and Curiosity

My decision to go into business alone was therefore rooted in a deep passion for new technologies and an incessant desire to discover and innovate. I wanted a space where my natural curiosity and desire for experimentation would be not only accepted but encouraged. Creating my own company was the only path that seemed to allow me to fully realize these aspirations.

A Visit to the Data Center: An Unexpected Turning Point

My first foray into a data center happened quite by chance, during my first internship in remote web development. This event, which seemed like fate, occurred in 1999, just before the creation of my company.

It all started one Saturday night on Caramail, a popular chat platform at the time. In a conversation with a young web developer, who was not even 18 years old and did not have a driver's license, I found an internship opportunity. After an unexpected meeting and a night out at a discotheque - a meeting made possible because I had a driver's license - he accepted me for an internship, although he himself worked from his parents' home and did not have a physical office.

Impressive Discovery at Claranet

Only two weeks later, I found myself in a Claranet data center in Paris, near the Élysée Palace. That's where his servers were located. At that time, I must admit that the world of data centers and what they involved did not really interest me. Everything operated under FreeBSD, a version of Linux that I found even more complex. I watched him type hundreds of lines of command in a terminal to run services like Apache, DNS, MySQL... For me, at that time, it all seemed like a "factory" too complicated. However, my colleague seemed to understand everything, while I understood absolutely nothing.

The Birth of Ligne Web Services (LWS) in 2003

Years have passed since my studies, and although my academic path did not meet all my expectations, I never stopped learning and developing outside of the school system. A decisive meeting with a Parisian entrepreneur from Marne-la-Vallée was a crucial turning point. He was looking for a developer to work on several major projects, including web portals, search engines, advertising networks, and directories.

Learning and Inspiration in Paris

Working with this entrepreneur gave me a valuable insight into the management of a structured and efficient sole proprietorship, especially in the dynamic and fast-paced context of Paris. Our exchanges were fruitful and I spent a lot of time in the capital working on his projects. I was impressed by the diversity of his activities, ranging from IT management to web creation, and by the breadth of his knowledge.

Confidence and Professional Recognition

This collaboration greatly strengthened my self-confidence. The entrepreneur recognized my development skills and entrusted me with significant projects, even introducing me to prestigious clients, such as personalities from rue du Faubourg Saint-Honoré and celebrities from the music world.

Stepping out of my comfort zone in this way was an enriching and formative experience.

Foundation of LWS and New Direction

A few months later, armed with these experiences and newfound confidence, I decided to create my own company, SARL LWS, which I domiciled in Paris, where I spent most of my time. This step marked a deeper commitment to my business, allowing me to devote more time and energy, and to fully exploit the opportunities available to me in the world of business and the Internet.

LWS: A Name Born from a Meeting and a Suggestion

The story of the name "LWS" begins with a chance encounter with an accountant in Champs-sur-Marne, introduced by a professional contact. When the time came to sign the company's statutes, I had the opportunity to discuss with the head of the accounting firm, a woman whose experience and insight were evident. She immediately raised a simple but crucial question: why choose "Ligne Web" as the company name, a name she found complicated to remember.

A Pertinent Suggestion

Without particular pretense about the name of my company, I explained that I sold web services, including hosting, domains, and website creation. Thoughtful, she suggested adding "Services" to the name to clarify the company's offering. To me, this seemed a minor detail at the time, as the essentials were in the domain names associated with my activity.

The Birth of LWS

She then proposed "Ligne Web Services" and suggested that the acronym "LWS" would be even more effective. I accepted this idea because for me, the name was secondary to the essence of the business. Thus, the name "LWS" was chosen almost by chance, but today it is under this name that my company is widely recognized.

The Official Creation of SARL LWS

A week after this enlightening discussion and decision on the name, SARL LWS with a capital of 1500 Euros was officially created. This moment marked the beginning of a new era for my business. With the formalization of LWS, I was ready to get serious and fully engage in the development of my web hosting business.

This step symbolized not only the realization of my past efforts but also the commitment to a promising and challenging future in the world of the Internet and technology.

Strategic Shift to Hosting and Domain Names

In 2003 and 2004, the web hosting landscape was bustling. Many hosts were appearing, and technologies were rapidly evolving. At that time, although my site A-a-hebergement.com was operational, I felt it was not reaching its full potential. The fear of losing everything and running out of clients if there was a major change in concept held me back. However, aware of the need to reinvent myself to stay competitive, I decided to create a new site: Hebergeur-Discount.com.

The Rapid Success of Hebergeur-Discount.com

This new platform marked a decisive turning point. Hebergeur-Discount.com enjoyed immediate and unexpected success, standing out clearly in the field of web hosting. This success validated my decision to specialize further in hosting and domain name management, a burgeoning sector essential for the online presence of businesses and individuals.

A New Era for LWS

The buzz around Hebergeur-Discount.com brought a new dynamic to my business. This success not only consolidated my position in the market but also opened the door to new opportunities and increased development. It was the start of an era where LWS affirmed itself as a major player in the web hosting universe.

Growth and Challenges: Managing the Success of Hebergeur-Discount.com

With the rapid increase in the number of clients and

recognition, Hebergeur-Discount.com began to face new challenges. Success had its price: more clients also meant more problems. I had reached the limit of what the Skyturn Antologic server could offer, and it became imperative to move to a more powerful dedicated server.

Transition to a Dedicated Server with IIS

This need for evolution led me to opt for a Windows Server, a decision influenced by my desire to continue supporting ASP and FrontPage. The switch from Apache to IIS (Internet Information Services) marked a significant transition in hosting management. For me, choosing a Windows server was obvious.

At that time, the idea of having to type hundreds of lines of code and compile manually on a Linux system seemed archaic. I was convinced that in the 2000s, user interfaces needed to evolve beyond command terminals to offer a more intuitive and accessible experience.

A New Technological Era

This transition to a Windows NT server with IIS represented a significant advancement for my business. It reflected my commitment to using technologies that, in my opinion, were at the forefront of innovation and ease of use. It was a decisive step, marking my adaptation to the changing demands of web hosting and my desire to provide my clients with the most advanced and practical solutions available.

THE ROOTS OF MY AVERSION TO TERMINAL CODING

To understand why I perceived lines of code in a terminal as obsolete and unattractive, it is essential to go back to my very first experiences in computing. These beginnings, marked by the use of a black and white Amstrad PC 1512, deeply influenced my vision of computing and its evolution.

First Steps in Computing: The Black and White PC 1512

My journey in the world of computing began at the age of 6, with a rather unexpected introduction. My uncle, a computer scientist, owned an Amstrad PC 1512 with a color screen, which greatly fascinated me. When my parents bought a PC 1512 for the family, they opted for a model with a black and white screen, a less expensive alternative. This version was less attractive compared to the CPC 6128s of my friends, who, in addition to their computers, often had video game consoles, adding even more color and interaction to their gaming experience.

The Constraints of DOS and the Discovery of Computing

Unlike my friends' computers, which offered a user-friendly BASIC environment and interactive games, my experience with the PC 1512 was focused on technical learning. Each use required the insertion of a DOS diskette, followed by a process to change diskettes and run programs. This early introduction to computing, although lacking the playful aspect of my friends' experiences, proved to be a solid foundation for my future skills.

Gratitude and Irony : My Uncle's Legacy

I am grateful to my uncle for introducing me to these computing concepts. However, there is a certain irony in thinking back to the advice he gave to my parents to opt for a PC 1512. What was at the time a boring and restrictive choice for a six-year-old child turned into an essential educational adventure, laying the groundwork for my passion and future career in the field of computing.

A Blessing in Disguise: Winter with the PC 1512

My childhood and youth in a small village, especially during the long winters where outdoor activities were limited, often found me in front of the Amstrad PC 1512 or occupied with my second passion: aeromodeling.

Those indoor days naturally steered me towards the computer as a primary source of entertainment and learning. Moreover, my regular visits to my uncle's house on Wednesdays offered fascinating glimpses into the world of computing through the eyes of my cousins.

Wednesdays of Learning and Inspiration

Particularly, my cousin Julien, who was the same age as me, greatly influenced me. We spent entire Wednesdays exploring the world of software on his computer. He had an impressive collection of programs, and unlike me, he knew how to program all of them. These moments were real intensive learning sessions. Julien was incredibly talented in design and was already using Photoshop on a PC 1512, creating images with pixel-perfect precision. His talent was undeniable, and his future in managing 3D effects for globally popular films confirmed it.

Discovering and Passion for Computing

These experiences with Julien motivated me to learn BASIC, master DOS commands, and fortunately, finally discover video games ! Although my family computer was less oriented towards entertainment, these experiences at my uncle's house allowed me to develop a keen interest in computing. They laid the foundations for my passion and future skills in this fascinating field.

2004 and Beyond : The Era of Windows NT Dedicated Servers

In 2004, my business took an important step by moving to dedicated Windows Server, still with a web interface developed by Skyturn. This change was necessary because Skyturn's initial solution (Antologic equivalent to VPS) had reached its performance limits. At that time, I was deeply convinced that the future of web hosting lay in fully interfaced and easy-to-administer solutions, like the one I had adopted.

Details: At the time, Skyturn's operating method was quite unusual and innovative. Instead of using Microsoft's standard solutions for Windows servers, such as IIS for the web server and Windows DNS server, Skyturn opted for a hybrid approach. They would install open-source software, such as Apache for the web server and Bind for DNS management, on Windows servers. This unique configuration was managed through a web control panel, developed with Windev. It is important to note that this control panel was designed for server management by the administrator and not for direct use by the end-user.

The Simplicity and Modernity of Windows IIS

When we made the decision to move to a dedicated server, a major technological change was also made: we chose to switch from Apache to Windows IIS for managing our web server. This transition was motivated by several key factors.

The switch from Apache to Windows IIS for web server management seemed to me a significant improvement. Setting up a website with Apache often required editing complex configuration files, while Windows IIS offered a much more user-friendly approach. A few clicks and filling in a few fields were enough to set up a website, a method I found both simple and modern. This ease of use was for me proof of technological evolution and better adaptability to user needs.

Appreciation in Hindsight

Over time, I've come to realize that my confidence in this approach may have been premature. Although the simplicity and efficiency of the Windows IIS interface were attractive, the future of web hosting turned out to be much more complex and diverse. This experience has been a valuable lesson: the importance of not relying solely on immediate ease of use, but also considering the flexibility and robustness of technological solutions in the long term.

Technical Challenges with Skyturn Solutions

As my business grew, the solutions provided by Skyturn began to present significant complications.

The process of migrating clients to new servers, especially

Windows IIS, proved to be complex. Particularly challenging was automating configurations on IIS, a task that was not straightforward at the time and often required manual intervention.

The Headache of Changing IP Addresses

To make matters worse, Skyturn imposed several rapid IP address changes. Today, the idea might seem amusing, but at the time, it was a true nightmare. Each IP change required manual revision of DNS configurations and adjustments in client domains, which were often scattered and managed independently. This era was characterized by a lack of automation, making each change both laborious and time-consuming.

Consequences on Business Management

I had invested a lot of energy in marketing and relied on supplier skills for development, system administration, and other technical aspects. The technical problems with Skyturn thus cost me precious time and forced me to slow down the acquisition of new clients in order to manage the technical aspects of the business. Several years elapsed during which I had to juggle between managing these issues and maintaining the quality of customer service.

Fear of Lack of Money and Determination to Succeed Alone

During this period of transition and growth for my business, I left my family home to settle in the Nancy region, attracted by a better ADSL connection. I also spent a lot of time in Paris, where my servers were located. Despite the challenges, the idea of borrowing money from a bank or looking for an investor was inconceivable to me. In hindsight, I think my decision was partly motivated by pride. After starting alone, with no one initially believing in my business, the idea of asking for help seemed like a step backward, a sign of weakness I refused to admit.

Family Influences and Cautious Management

My childhood was marked by constant discussions about money within my family. My parents, not having abundant financial resources, often spoke of money, instilling in me a keen awareness of its value. Although I never lacked anything and was happy, I did not have access to the brands or luxuries that some of my peers had. Instead, I had a computer, which, over time, proved to be a much greater advantage. These experiences shaped my relationship with money: I have always tended to manage my finances with extreme caution, a habit deeply ingrained in me from an early age.

Unlike my own upbringing, I chose not to reproduce the same relationship with money for my children. My goal has been to keep them away from financial concerns, thus allowing them to fully dedicate themselves to discovering and exploring their passions. The idea is to give them the opportunity to find a fulfilling professional activity, just as I found mine, even if it was by chance. I am aware that this often involves a bit of luck, or the need to provoke it. This approach, and the reflections it raises about financial education, could be a topic I might explore in more detail in another book.

The End of the Skyturn Era and the Transition to Ecritel

After a few years, the news came: Skyturn, the provider I had relied on so much, closed its doors and was acquired by Ecritel, a company with a more solid structure and more resources. However, I had not waited for this eventuality to diversify my options. I had already acquired other servers from different suppliers, anticipating a possible need for transition.

The Arrival of My First Employee in the Early 2000s

In the early 2000s, an important turning point occurred in my company with the arrival of my first employee. He was a friend with whom I had studied in BTS. His integration into the company marked the beginning of a new phase of development. His main mission was to manage the relationship with our clients, a crucial role for the support and growth of the company.

Division of Roles and Multitasking

At that time, the company's structure was simple, but effective. My employee focused on customer service while I handled almost all other aspects of the company: server administration, sales, development, and general organization. I was involved in every facet of the business, motivated by my perception that everything seemed simple and achievable.

Boundless Energy and Commitment

I did not measure the time spent working on these different aspects, as my passion for what I was doing made these efforts seem almost effortless. This period was characterized by total commitment and overflowing energy, fueled by the belief that I could handle everything alone. It was not just a matter of control, but also a manifestation of my enthusiasm and dedication to my business and its success.

Multifaceted Role as Founder and Technician

When my company had only one employee, my responsibilities were vast and varied. I was in charge of creating and maintaining the website, designing order forms, and implementing the first automations for deliveries. At the same time,

I developed the first versions of the LWS Panel, the control panel intended for our clients. This initiative was all the more crucial as at that time, reliable and comprehensive control panels for clients were rare or nonexistent.

Server Migration and Maintenance

This period also coincided with the migration of some of our servers from Skyturn to our new data center space provider, CTN1. I personally managed the physical installation of the machines, which involved regular trips to Paris to ensure their maintenance and setup. This transition was not only technical but also logistical, requiring constant presence and meticulous attention.

Intense Work Pace

The pace of work during these months was intense. My days were long, and the tasks were relentless. I limited myself to about six hours of sleep per night, seven days a week. This period of my life was characterized by total dedication to the company, a passion for the work accomplished, and a rhythm that bordered on the incessant.

Nonexistent Vacations and Commitment to Customer Support

In those early years, the concept of vacations was foreign to me. When my sole employee took his leave, I took over customer support. These periods were particularly intense but extremely rewarding. Answering the phone, understanding the problems and needs of the clients provided me with extreme motivation. I have always loved a challenge, and these direct interactions with clients only increased my commitment.

Continuous Development and Rapid Improvement

From 6 pm, when the calls diminished, I would dive into

development and bug fixing reported by clients. My natural impatience and willingness to act quickly often pushed me to work late into the night. This haste, although sometimes a handicap, was a central element of my modus operandi. My goal was to provide services that were not only reliable but also easy for our clients to use.

Creation of a Memorable Slogan

It was in this context of hard work and dedication to customer service that our iconic slogan was born: "Web hosting accessible to all." This slogan perfectly reflected our mission: to make web hosting affordable and easy to manage for everyone. It was conceived during this period of intense work and has never changed since, embodying the very essence of our company's approach and values.

REFLECTING ON THE TECHNICAL CHALLENGES

WITH WINDOWS SERVER

*A*lways around 2003-2005, this transition was not smooth. I had chosen to remain loyal to Windows Server technology to facilitate the migration, but this decision turned out to be problematic. The OS, once perceived as a simple and modern solution, gradually became a real nightmare due to stability issues and market evolution. The demand for ASP was decreasing, FrontPage had become obsolete, and managing PHP on Windows was causing increasing security and compatibility problems.

Scaling Back Business Activities

Faced with these technical difficulties, I had to make the tough decision to scale back my business activities to avoid being overwhelmed. This involved putting a brake on acquiring new clients and focusing on managing existing problems. This period was marked by a need for technical and strategic reevaluation, forcing me to rethink the infrastructure and services I was offering.

Confronting the Complexities of Web Hosting

Over time, it became clear that selling a web hosting service was much more complex than managing a simple e-commerce site with the delivery of physical products. What had started as a relatively simple technical task to run a website had turned into an entanglement of complications. Every aspect of web hosting, from DNS to security, including PHP, MySQL, network management, and web servers, was modernizing and, at the same time, becoming more complex.

The Limitations of Windows in Web Hosting

The use of Windows Server, which I had initially perceived as a practical solution, proved to be an ill-suited choice in the face of these evolutions. This technology was overtaken by the rapid advances and growing demands of the field. Managing a mail server under Windows, for example, had become a daunting task, overwhelmed by spam and reliability issues. The limitations of mail server software, IIS, anti-spam solutions, PHP and MySQL adaptation, licenses, backups, as well as reliability problems of the NTFS file system with thousands of files and folders, had become a burden.

Significant Time Devoted to Technical Management

All these technical complications forced me to dedicate a significant amount of time to stabilizing the infrastructure, often to the detriment of the commercial development of the business. My desire not to disappoint my current clients and my stubbornness in personally managing these problems, while juggling other aspects of the business, significantly slowed my development.

In hindsight, I realize that a different approach, technologically more reliable, could have propelled me to the rank of a market leader in web hosting, not only in France but potentially far beyond.

The Impact of a Technological Misjudgment

The trajectory of my business was profoundly influenced by an initial misjudgment regarding the technology to adopt. Seduced by the user-friendly interface of Windows and IIS, I made a choice that seemed wise at the time. However, this choice turned out to be limiting in the face of the rapid and complex evolution of the web hosting domain. The immediate ease provided by these technologies masked their long-term shortcomings.

Lack of Flexibility and Fear of Change

Over time, it became clear that I had not sufficiently considered the need for more flexible and robust technology. I lacked the courage to make a radical change, moving away from Windows to explore other potentially more suitable technological solutions. Moreover, I did not seek to surround myself with experts who could have guided me towards better technological decisions.

Consequences for Business Growth

This reluctance to evolve and adapt had a direct effect on the growth of my business. By remaining attached to a technology that no longer met market demands, I inadvertently slowed down the development and expansion of my activity. This experience was an important lesson on the importance of adaptability and informed decision-making in the technology field.

2007: The First Steps Towards a New Chapter

The year 2007 marked the beginning of a series of significant changes in my company. Despite the challenges encountered with Windows servers, I had not ceased to evolve my business. One of the major developments was the expansion of the domain name management part of my business.

Development of the Domain Name Sector

I focused my efforts on developing the domain name branch, an area that aligned more with my skills and interests in web development. To support this growth, I hired several people to strengthen the support and development team, and I undertook the necessary steps to become an official domain registrar.

Preference for Web Development

My penchant for web development, rather than pure server administration, guided this decision.

Becoming a domain registrar represented an opportunity to focus more on programming and web development aspects, areas where I felt more comfortable and passionate. It was a natural step that combined my development skills with a growing market opportunity.

Strategic Transition to Apache and Linux

In the years following 2007, I developed a clear plan to gradually phase out IIS in favor of Apache on Linux. This decision marked a radical change from my initial preference for Windows. Although I had an aversion to Linux and its many distributions, the need to adapt to technological and market requirements motivated this turn.

Choosing the Right Linux Distribution

The question of which Linux distribution to choose arose. With a multitude of options available, each with its own characteristics and benefits, the decision was not easy. However, after thorough research, exhaustive reading, and numerous tests, the choice was made for Debian. This decision was guided by its reputation for stability, security, and reliability, essential qualities for an effective web hosting service.

A Process of Learning and Recruitment

This period was also marked by a significant learning process. I spent many hours studying books and online resources to better understand and master Linux. Concurrently, recruiting talent familiar with this environment became a priority to ensure that the team had the necessary skills to manage this transition and make the most of the possibilities offered by Linux and Apache.

The Dilemma Between Debian and CentOS

When it came time to choose a Linux distribution for the company, a lively discussion ensued between me and my system administrators. Initially, I was leaning towards CentOS, a platform widely used by web hosts and renowned for the longevity of its versions. The prospect of being able to maintain an operating system for seven years without requiring a complete reinstallation seemed particularly advantageous from a managerial perspective, minimizing interruptions and time losses.

Decision Making and Listening to Experts

However, I had to remind myself that, although I personally preferred Debian, I should not be the sole decision-maker in this crucial technical choice. It was essential to listen to and trust the expertise of my collaborators, the system administrators, who were the real experts in this domain. Eventually, we opted for Debian, a decision guided by their recommendations and knowledge.

Validation of the Choice Over Time

In hindsight, this decision proved to be wise. The CentOS project underwent changes and uncertainties over time, making the platform less attractive than it initially was. This experience reinforced my belief that listening to and collaborating with the experts on my team is essential for making informed decisions, particularly in technical areas where my own expertise may be limited.

The Decision to Collaborate with CTN1 and TeleCity

Following the closure of services offered by Skyturn and its absorption by Ecritel around 2006, I decided not to continue with them, but rather to turn to another company with installations at TeleCity. This new company, La Compagnie des Télécoms Numériques 1 (CTN1), attracted me with its impressive capital and a name that inspired trust. Their competitive offers and apparent quality of service seemed ideal for what I was looking for: a chance to focus on software development while delegating data center management and telecom operations.

The Complexities of the Web Hosting Business

To fully grasp the stakes of this transition, it is important to understand the intrinsic complexity of the web hosting business. A web host requires a data center operating without interruption, with foolproof climate, electrical, and security infrastructure. In 2005, standards and technologies were not as advanced as they are today, making the operation of a data center even more delicate.

Technical and Material Requirements

This is in addition to the need for specialized and high-performance computer servers capable of handling constant and intense web traffic. Network connectivity had to be impeccable, offering optimal connection speed and reliability to the entire world. Finally, it was crucial to be equipped with cutting-edge software to ensure a quality user experience and efficient service management.

Delegation and Focus on Software

By choosing to collaborate with CTN1 and take advantage of their installations at TeleCity, my goal was to lighten the burden of daily management of these complex technical aspects. This decision allowed me to delegate the network routing and server room part to experts while focusing on the development and improvement of the software aspects of my business, an area where I could add the most value.

CTN1's Innovative Appeal: Mastery of IPv4 and IPv6 Technologies

In my search for a new partner to host my servers, CTN1 stood out as a particularly attractive option. What particularly appealed to me was their technological advancement, notably their mastery of IPv4 and IPv6 protocols. At the time, competence in managing IPv6 was exceptional and rare, signaling a company at the forefront of innovation in the telecommunications and networking field.

The Decision to Collaborate with CTN1

Convinced by their expertise and their ability to manage these advanced technologies, I decided to place several servers with them. This decision was based on the trust that CTN1 could not only meet the current hosting needs of my business but also that they were well-positioned to adapt to future internet network evolutions.

A Partnership Geared Towards the Future

By integrating my servers at CTN1, I hoped not only to benefit from a robust and reliable infrastructure but also from a platform ready to embrace future technological advances. Their expertise in IPv4 and IPv6 represented a significant advantage to keep my business competitive and at the forefront of technology in a constantly evolving market.

The Failure of the Collaboration with CTN1

The collaboration with CTN1, which initially presented itself as a promising opportunity, turned out to be a resounding failure. This choice, which I believed to be judicious at the time, ultimately led to a notable slowdown of my business. Problems began to emerge quickly, revealing technical shortcomings, particularly in networking, at CTN1.

Technical Difficulties and an Inevitable Break

As the problems accumulated, it became increasingly evident that CTN1 was not meeting the quality and reliability standards I demanded for my services. This realization ultimately led to the difficult decision to end our partnership. However, the separation from CTN1 did not occur smoothly.

The Complexity of Server Recovery

The phase of separation was particularly challenging. Recovering all our servers hosted with them turned into a real puzzle, scattered with obstacles and complications. This experience was a true obstacle course, requiring great determination and meticulous management to ensure the smooth transfer of our precious material resources.

Mixed Experience with CTN1 and a Positive Nod to Telecity

Without dwelling on the details of my collaboration with CTN1 – a subject on which I have my personal opinions – it is important to mention the positive experience I had with the Telecity data center. Despite the difficulties encountered with CTN1, the data center itself and its staff proved to be of great help and support.

Appreciation for Telecity Data Center

The Telecity data center was, without a doubt, one of my favorites. The professionalism, efficiency, and friendliness of the staff, particularly the receptionist, contributed greatly to making my experience pleasant and productive. Their assistance and support were invaluable in managing the challenges related to hosting my servers.

Pleasant Reunion at Equinix

A few years later, I had the pleasure of meeting the same reception person again, this time at Equinix, another data center. This unexpected encounter was a pleasant moment, reinforcing my appreciation for the competent and dedicated individuals working in these facilities crucial to the web hosting world.

The Disappearance of CTN1: The End of a Digital Giant

It is worth noting that, a few years after our separation, CTN1 disappeared. What had seemed to be a digital giant with enormous potential ultimately did not endure over time. Their closure, which occurred in a rapidly evolving technological context, underscores the volatility and complexity of the web hosting sector. This abrupt end marked the conclusion of a chapter in the digital hosting domain and served as a reminder of the importance of stability and reliability in choosing business partners.

The Lesson from the Failure of Digital Giants

The story of CTN1 and Skyturn, with their respective disappearances despite significant financial resources, taught me a crucial lesson: having a lot of money does not guarantee longevity over time. At the time, these companies had resources far superior to mine – more funds, more technicians, and access to more advanced technologies. Yet, despite these apparent advantages, they did not survive in the long run.

Management and Strategy: Keys to Longevity

This observation made me realize that success in the field of web hosting does not rely solely on financial capital but also and above all on effective management and a well-thought-out strategy. The disappearance of these companies, despite their financial and technological assets, highlights the importance of a long-term vision, a good understanding of the market, and adaptability to the sector's constant changes.

Anticipation and Accreditation: The Case of Namebay

This reflection is also relevant when I think about my first domain name provider, Namebay, before I became an accredited registrar. Their journey, as well as the reasons that led me to seek independent accreditation, will be detailed later. This step was another example highlighting the importance of anticipating market developments and making informed strategic decisions for the sustainable growth of the business.

LWS's Initial Steps in Domain Name Management with Namebay

In the beginning, before becoming an independent registrar, LWS collaborated with Namebay for domain name management. Namebay, one of the first registrars based in Monaco, offered an advanced technological solution through its API, enabling automatic domain reservations for our clients. This collaboration played a key role in our early years, allowing us to offer efficient and automated domain name services to our clients.

Evolution and Changes

Since then, Namebay has undergone changes, including being acquired by Nameshield. As they are still in operation, I will not elaborate on their current situation or our past relationship. What I can assert is that this experience with Namebay was an important step in our journey, providing us with valuable insights and preparing us to become an autonomous registrar.

The Impact of this Collaboration

This initial period with Namebay marked significant learning for LWS, teaching us the subtleties of domain name management and the importance of effective technological integration. This laid the groundwork for our future evolution as an independent registrar, allowing us to offer our clients a more complete and personalized service.

2007: A Strategic Turning Point with SIVIT

In 2007, although my company had a satisfactory number of clients, I was aware of a technical limit preventing us from further increasing our clientele. After two successive failures with data centers, I found myself in a delicate situation, all the more so as I observed competitors, notably the French leader in the sector, progressing rapidly and gaining a considerable lead.

REFLECTION ON CREDIT AND INVESTMENT

*D*espite these challenges, I remained hesitant about taking on debt or opening up my company's capital. In a technology world that was constantly changing, where nothing seemed stable and each week brought its own set of innovations and updates, this caution seemed justified, especially given the relative reliability of servers at the time.

COLLABORATION WITH SIVIT: A Fortunate Encounter

It was in this context that I came across SIVIT, a hosting provider larger than my company. This encounter, which happened by chance, paved the way for a successful collaboration. SIVIT had an excellent reputation, a serious team, and a very open technical approach, qualities that immediately appealed to me. We hit it off right away.

A Reliable Infrastructure and Quality Support

SIVIT operated server spaces at Red BUS Interhouse, near

La Défense, a leading data center with a concierge service available 24/7, in addition to SIVIT's technical support. This high-quality infrastructure and level of support were exactly what my company needed to stabilize and look to the future with more confidence.

Expansion and New Challenges

Around 2008, my company went through a significant expansion phase. I found new offices in Epinal, a change that symbolized the growth and evolution of the company. This period was also marked by the recruitment of new collaborators, a sign that the company was structuring and strengthening itself.

Working with Fewer Constraints

With these new spaces and an expanded team, we began to work with fewer operational constraints. This positive dynamic allowed us to look to the future with more optimism and to plan the development of the company more strategically.

Transition to a Linux Environment

However, this growth period was accompanied by significant technical challenges. One of the main projects was to finalize and launch our offers based 100% on Linux, while planning the gradual phasing out of our Windows park. This transition was a daunting task, involving migrating all our clients to the new environment. It was a time-consuming undertaking but necessary to align our infrastructure and services with current technological standards and market expectations.

The Era of Virtualization and Multi-Core CPUs

The advent of virtualization was a revelation in the world of web hosting, a technological advance that synchronized with the increasing accessibility of multi-core CPUs. This innovation represented an exceptional opportunity for my company, allowing us to optimize our resources and offer more efficient and flexible services to our clients.

Discovery of SuperMicro: An Economical and Custom Solution

Simultaneously, faced with reliability issues with servers from some well-established brands, I discovered the Super-Micro brand. This discovery, thanks to a distributor who had been soliciting us for years, turned out to be a godsend. SuperMicro offered less expensive solutions than its competitors while allowing for the creation of custom servers that precisely met our needs, without any superfluous features.

Prudent Investment Management

Being unable to invest in a large number of servers in advance due to budgetary constraints, SuperMicro proved to be the ideal partner. Their flexible and economical approach matched our financial situation and our strategy of measured growth perfectly.

Challenges of Migration and Lessons Learned

The period of migration from CTN1 to Sivit was particularly trying. Moving the servers, the necessary reconfigurations, especially of the DNS in a context where we were not yet a registrar, posed a real challenge. Although this transition temporarily affected our commercial reputation, it taught me important lessons about the technical and operational management of a web hosting company, strengthening our resilience and ability to overcome complex technical challenges.

INCREASED COMPETITION AND NEW CHALLENGES

*I*n 2009, as the web hosting market evolved, the competition became increasingly intense. Globally structured groups began to establish themselves in the French market, coming with resources far superior to those of LWS. This period was also marked by numerous consolidations in the sector, heralding major changes for the years to come.

The acquisition of Sivit by Nerim

Our server space provider, Sivit, was not spared by this wave of consolidations. It was acquired by Nerim, a larger network operator (which, in turn, would later be acquired by Bouygues Telecom). This acquisition had direct and significant repercussions for LWS. Nerim decided to move all of Sivit's equipment to another data center, this time at Equinix in Saint-Denis.

Moving to Equinix: A logistical challenge with the

support of Nerim

The move of our infrastructure to Equinix represented a major logistical challenge for LWS. At that time, we had accumulated a significant amount of equipment, making this migration much more complex and delicate than those we had undertaken before. Planning and executing this massive equipment transfer required meticulous organization and attention, especially in our effort to minimize disruptions for our customers.

Effective collaboration with Nerim

Fortunately, we benefited from invaluable assistance from Nerim during this process. Their support was a key factor in the smooth running of the move. Thanks to their help and effective coordination, the transfer to Equinix went generally well, despite the complexity of the operation. This collaboration demonstrated the importance of reliable and competent partners in managing the logistical challenges of such magnitude.

Unexpected reunion at Equinix

The move to Equinix reserved a pleasant surprise for us: the rediscovery of a familiar face at the reception of the data center. This person, whom we had known when she worked at TeleCity, was not only very friendly but also always ready to help.

A human link in a technological world

These reunions added a welcome human touch to the entire moving process. Finding an acquaintance in an environment as technical and specialized as that of Equinix strengthened the sense of continuity and community in the sometimes impersonal world of data centers. Her willingness and efficiency during our interventions at the data center greatly facilitated our transition and contributed to creating a positive and collaborative atmosphere.

The value of relationships in the web hosting sector

This experience highlighted the importance of human relationships in the web hosting sector. Although technology is at the heart of our business, human interactions remain essential for smooth and efficient operation. The presence of this familiar person at Equinix was a valuable reminder that behind every piece of equipment and every line of code, there are dedicated and skilled individuals who contribute to the success of our business.

The Data Center: A World of Magic and Rigor

VISITING a data center is an experience that is both magical and strange. 58romm y first foray into one of these nerve centers of the internet to my visit at Equinix Saint-Denis, years have passed, and my perception of these places has evolved. A data center is more than just a storage location : it is a vital ecosystem for the internet. Without them, the internet as we know it would not exist, a reality often unknown to the general public.

FIRST IMPRESSIONS and Evolution

DURING MY FIRST VISITS, I was struck by the austerity and the impressive aspect of data centers. These places, where technology meets high-level security, can seem intimidating at first glance.

. . .

The identification and security protocols are rigorous, from access to the parking lot to the computer rooms, with constant monitoring.

The Experience at Equinix Saint-Denis

At Equinix Saint-Denis, one of the largest data centers in France, this impression of austerity and rigor is even more pronounced. After passing through multiple levels of security, one walks through long corridors before reaching the computer rooms, each protected by secure access. This experience underscores the seriousness and importance of these facilities in managing and protecting our digital infrastructure.

Morning Visits to the Data Center : A Solitary and Intense Experience

My early days at LWS were punctuated by early morning trips to data centers in the Paris region. I would often leave around 4 a.m. to avoid traffic jams, arriving at the data center around 9 a.m. after a solitary drive on the highway. These visits required rigor and sustained attention: once in the server room, I found myself alone amidst a constant hum, surrounded by thousands of servers.

A Surreal and Demanding Atmosphere

In these rooms, where the noise of the servers fills the space, concentration is paramount. Setting up, connecting equipment, and starting work requires the ability to remain focused despite the isolation and surrounding noise. Initially, these interventions aroused in me a certain apprehension. The atmosphere is singular : often deserted, the server room offers almost total solitude, rarely interrupted by the presence of other people.

Nights at the Data Center : A Sci-Fi Setting

Nocturnal interventions add an additional dimension to the experience. Imagine being in the middle of thousands of servers in a deafening noise, alone at 3 a.m. It's a world far from the friendly atmosphere of a nightclub, more akin to a sci-fi setting. These moments spent in data centers have been significant experiences, teaching me to deal with isolation and pressure in a demanding and unconventional environment.

A Surreal and Demanding Atmosphere, Between Extreme Heat and Cold

THE EXPERIENCE in the server rooms, where the noise of the machines dominates, demands unwavering concentration. Installing and connecting equipment in this environment also means learning to manage isolation and noise. Initially, I felt a certain apprehension about this almost total solitude, seldom interrupted by other people.

DIFFICULT CLIMATIC CONDITIONS

IN ADDITION TO THE NOISE, the climatic conditions in these rooms were extreme. It was very cold, especially because of the air blowing from the floor, while behind the servers, the temperature soared. This alternation between icy cold and stifling heat was ideal for getting sick. Old generation data centers operated this way, without the separation into hot and cold corridors found in modern facilities.

THE EVOLUTION of Data Centers in 20 Years

THESE CONDITIONS REFLECT the significant evolution of data centers over the past 20 years. From one generation to the next, cooling methods and space management have radically changed, moving from open rooms to more efficient containment systems. An entire chapter could be dedicated to these changes, illustrating the extent of innovations and technical improvements in the field of data centers

A STABILIZATION AND A MATURELY CONSIDERED GROWTH

Around 2012, my company seemed to finally find its cruising speed. We had acquired more servers and expanded our team. Before this year, I had moments of doubt, wondering how to catch up and gain recognition in a highly competitive sector. I was aware of possible solutions, but had chosen not to implement them previously.

The Temptation of Paris and the Choice of Quality of Life

One of these solutions would have been to move the entire business to Paris, where I had an extensive network and could easily have recruited experts to join LWS. However, I chose to start a family and prioritize a less stressful environment than Paris. Life in the capital, with its frenetic pace and constant traffic jams, did not match the work-life balance I was looking for.

Refusal of Excessive Financial Risks

Another option would have been to build a server room in Épinal, but the costs associated with installing optical fibers were prohibitive. This path would have required either a major investment or a significant loan, thus increasing financial risks. I decided not to go down this route, preferring a more cautious and less risky approach.

2013 and Beyond: Towards an Improved and Diversified Service Offering

After 2013, the evolution of my company was marked by significant improvements in both our services and our team. This period was characterized by continuous growth and consolidation of our reputation in the web hosting market.

Launch of the First VPS

In 2014, we took an important step by launching our first VPS (Virtual Private Servers). This move towards virtualization was a technological revolution for me, offering flexibility and possibilities far superior to those of traditional dedicated servers. I was particularly excited to work in this virtualization environment, convinced of its immense potential.

Becoming a Domain Registrar: A Key Milestone

Another crucial milestone was reached when we became a domain registrar, not just for .FR domains. We extended our accreditation to the most popular extensions like .COM, .NET, and .ORG.

This step required a much more complex accreditation procedure and represented a major challenge for the company.

Thanks to the Team

I would like to express my gratitude to all my collaborators for their dedication and hard work during this period. Without their support and commitment, overcoming these key stages would have been much more difficult. Their ability to adapt to changes, meet challenges, and not slow down in the face of obstacles was essential for the success and continuous growth of the company.

A New Era with Larger Offices and Fiber Optic Connectivity

The year 2015 marked a pivotal period for my company, characterized by significant changes in our work environment. We moved to larger offices, a tangible sign of our growth and development. This move to Golbey represented much more than just a change of address; it symbolized a new stage in the company's evolution.

The Arrival of Fiber: A Catalyst for Acceleration

With the move came the installation of fiber optic connectivity in our new premises. This technological advancement was a true catalyst, significantly accelerating our communication capabilities and operational efficiency. High-speed connectivity opened up new possibilities in terms of service management, collaboration, and innovation.

Simplification and Some Challenges in Golbey

The transfer to Golbey led to a notable simplification of our operations. The layout of the new offices, combined with improved connectivity, facilitated the daily work of the team and contributed to a better work atmosphere. However, this change was not without its challenges. Adapting to a new environment and managing the move while maintaining service continuity for our clients required considerable effort and meticulous planning.

Network Management and IPv4 Address Challenges

The relocation of our server park was a turning point, pushing me to take a greater interest in network management. Until then, I had delegated this task to a more significant network infrastructure provider, not seeing a direct added value for our shared web hosting activity. Our business model did not require thousands of physical servers to host a large number of sites, so IP address management seemed relatively simple: we requested a certain number of IP addresses from our network carrier and managed the rest internally.

The IPv4 Address Problem

However, a major complication arose: if there was a problem with the network carrier, they would retain the IPv4 addresses. This scenario would involve changing IP addresses for our servers, a task that, although simplified by years of experience and our domain registrar status, remained significant. In 2015, changing IP addresses was no longer a Herculean task for LWS, thanks to our software and logistical expertise, but it was still a challenge not to be underestimated.

Advantages in Logistics and Software

Although we did not have our data center, our expertise in logistics and software placed us in an advantageous position. As a domain registrar, we had greater ease and flexibility in managing these IP changes. This period underscored the importance of autonomous network management and reinforced our ability to navigate the complexities of the web hosting world.

The IPv4 Scam and Strategy Change

My naivety and honesty led to a late realization: managing IPv4 addresses was far from as simple as I had imagined. The standard procedure involved requesting these addresses from RIPE NCC, the regulatory body in Europe, and theoretically, returning them once they were no longer needed. But in practice, this procedure turned out to be more complex and less transparent.

Acquisition of Our IPv4 Addresses

In this new context, I made the strategic decision to request our IPv4 addresses, learning from our previous experiences. However, RIPE's rules had tightened, making it more complicated to obtain a sufficient number of IPv4 addresses. Despite the high requirements for justification, we obtained the necessary number of IP addresses without seeking to accumulate more than our actual need. This honest and prudent approach reflected our commitment not to repeat past mistakes and to ensure transparent and responsible management of our network resources.

IPv4s: Between Shortage and Speculation

The IPv4 scam begins with the reality of a limited and saturated market. By 2022, the situation was such that IPv4 addresses, technically limited in number, had become a scarce commodity. IPv6, supposed to replace IPv4, had not yet led to a mass abandonment of the latter. Instead of returning unused IPv4s to RIPE or their regional equivalents, many providers and market players chose to sell them at exorbitant prices. An IPv4 address could thus cost about 50 dollars, turning what was originally a resource without intrinsic value into a speculative asset.

Missed Anticipation and Maintained Ethics

I admit neither anticipating this situation nor choosing to participate in this speculation. Unlike some large hosts who had stockpiled millions of IPv4s as early as the 2000s-2010s,

LWS had not accumulated such a stock, preferring a more honest approach consistent with our values. If I had requested a million IPv4s back then, it's likely that I would have gotten them without difficulty, and the value of LWS would have been considerably increased. But this approach was not aligned with our company ethics.

Working Harder to Compensate and Invest in IPv6

Faced with this shortage, we had to redouble our efforts and gradually purchase IPv4s to support our growth. At the same time, we fully embraced IPv6, thus becoming one of the best-rated hosts in this area.

This experience reinforced my belief that difficulties should never be a hindrance but rather a driver for innovation and adaptation.

A REWARDING EVOLUTION: FROM MY BEGINNINGS TO TODAY

Reflecting on my beginnings, I realize the distance I've traveled with LWS. Each morning, as I go to my company, I feel the same joy and enthusiasm as on the first day. This adventure has taught me countless lessons, both professionally and personally. The growth of LWS, although not having reached the first place in the market, is for me a source of immense pride.

LWS: An Authentic and Independent Company

What matters most to me is that LWS remains true to its original vision: to simplify a sector that is moving towards increasing complexity. Despite not being the market leader, LWS has retained its essence: a 100% independent company, away from the turbulence often associated with acquisitions and the involvement of investment funds. This independence was a deliberate choice, guided by my desire to preserve the soul and core values of the company.

Anticipation and Precautions with New Data Centers

BECOMING A WEB HOSTING PROVIDER

Faced with concerning signs from Sivit since its acquisition by Nerim, I made the proactive decision to diversify our facilities. With the aim of reducing travel to Paris and optimizing our infrastructure, we established a new partnership with a company located in Nancy. We chose Adista, a next-generation data center that offered both proximity and technological excellence.

The collaboration with Adista marked a turning point in our strategy. Although I had known them for some time, I was not initially completely convinced by their first infrastructure. However, around 2015, the situation had evolved for both them and us. Their new infrastructure met our high requirements, and I quickly found myself in tune with their technical team and their leaders. This collaboration with Adista allowed us to adopt a totally different work approach, aligned with our ambitions and our vision of web hosting service.

Organization of Servers in a Data Center

Software suitable for managing servers in a Data Center were scarce or prohibitively expensive in the early 2000s. In the beginning, managing a few servers was easily done with a basic database. I quickly set up a simple interface, designed with a few lines of PHP code and a MySQL database, to meet these initial needs. However, this initial solution quickly proved insufficient as our activities expanded. Managing IP addresses, securing VLANs (virtual networks), and other technical challenges added to the complexity of the task.

Faced with these challenges, innovation and engineering became essential to manage hundreds of servers effectively, allowing smooth collaboration within our infrastructure. Even today, the absence of tools perfectly suited to these specific needs has led us to develop our own custom solutions, tailored to our unique services. This ability to adapt and innovate has been fundamental in competing with much larger and better-equipped companies and has played a key role in the success of LWS.

Modernization and Continuous Improvement

Since 2016, LWS has been constantly modernizing and innovating. Our services have become more and more efficient, thus meeting the changing needs of our clients while remaining at the forefront of technology. This dynamic of continuous improvement reflects our commitment to offering the best to our customers, while staying true to our original mission: making web hosting accessible and simple for everyone.

Independence as a Driver of Innovation and Success

Independence has always been a central element of LWS's strategy, but it comes with its own set of challenges. To compete with the giants of the industry, often publicly traded or part of large groups, we had to adopt an innovative approach, find shortcuts, and work in an unconventional way. And above all, it means working more. Many wonder about the secret of LWS's success: the answer lies in the fact that nothing is left to chance. I dedicate many hours to this work, which is also a passion, and I surround myself only with people who share the philosophy and ethics of the company.

Strategic Technical Choices Pay Off

1. **Independent Domain Registrar**: Being an independent domain registrar is a significant fact for LWS. Unlike many others, we are not resellers. French registrars of our size are rare, and we are among the first, thanks to our perseverance and the

expansion of our accreditations. Although complex to manage, this activity is masterfully controlled by our team.

2. **The LWS Panel**: We are one of the few hosts that do not rely on paid third-party solutions like cPanel or Plesk. Creating and maintaining an in-house web control panel is a considerable challenge, but it also offers unique advantages, which I will return to in more detail.

3. **Independent Network and Infrastructure**: Even without owning our own data center, we have developed a solid network infrastructure. With our own IP addresses and our status as a network operator (ASN), we have the flexibility to place our servers where we want and to manage routing transparently.

2016-2020: A Period of Technical Challenges and Strategic Investment

Between 2016 and 2020, prior to the outbreak of the Covid-19 crisis, LWS went through a period of intense technical challenges while continuing to develop. The adoption of virtualization and the switch to SSD storage brought greater flexibility and speed to our services, but they also required in-depth expertise.

Technical Advances with Underlying Challenges

On the surface, our web hosting, email services, and domains seemed to evolve smoothly. However, beneath this facade of simplicity, numerous internal technical challenges had to be overcome. These challenges are common to all hosts, but the way a small team like ours manages them compared to a team of hundreds of people is vastly different.

Growth and Reinvestment in LWS

During this period, LWS was not just a growing company but also a continuous investment for me. The company, which started with a capital of 1,500 €, saw its capital increase to over 500,000 €, held by the LWS group, which itself has a capital of 1,000,000 €. All resources and profits generated over the years have been reinvested in the company, illustrating my commitment to supporting its growth and strengthening its position in the French-speaking market.

Holding Our Own Against Market Leaders

This strategy of continuous reinvestment was crucial to allow us to hold our own against the top players in the French-speaking market. It is clear that reaching such a level of competitiveness requires not just ingenuity and dedication, but also significant financial investment.

Development and Capabilities of the LWS Panel

Creating and managing a web control panel is a significant challenge, especially when competing with established solutions like cPanel or Plesk, which rely on hundreds of developers. So, how has LWS, with its more limited resources, managed to develop its own control panel? Is it less efficient or less comprehensive?

A Complex and Evolving Panel

Far from it. The LWS Panel was designed to be intuitive for novices and advanced enough for experts. It has evolved over the years to offer a range of features that compete with the best in the market. Thousands of reviews on Trustpilot and Google attest to its quality and efficiency.

Rich and Diverse Features

Among its many features, the LWS Panel offers a shell terminal, an application auto-installer, a web firewall manager, mail distribution tracking, a multi-IP manager, and a daily backup system for mail, web, and databases. Furthermore, its file manager is of exceptional quality, and the WordPress Manager is an invaluable tool for managing and securing WordPress sites.

An Interface Designed for All

The UX design of the LWS Panel has been carefully thought out so that users, whether novices or experts, can easily navigate the interface. This includes advanced cache management, customizable anti-malware and anti-spam settings, as well as a variety of PHP versions. The panel is not just comprehensive for web hosting, but also for managing VPS servers and online storage solutions.

REFLECTION ON THE EARLY YEARS OF LWS: LEARNINGS AND EVOLUTION

*I*n the early years of LWS, I made mistakes that ultimately taught me a lot. My initial approach to technology, especially the choice between Windows and Linux, and my tendency to want to manage everything on my own, limited the company and slowed our progress. Additionally, my naivety and excessive optimism sometimes hindered our ability to deal with the realities of the web hosting market.

The Importance of Team and Collaboration

However, these challenges have been powerful catalysts for my creativity and motivation. They taught me the crucial importance of surrounding myself with a reliable and competent team. The saying 'Alone we go faster, together we go further' really resonated with me. It's crucial to thank my team for their unwavering support: their contribution has been a determining factor in the growth and ongoing success of LWS.

Lessons Learned and Personal Growth

These experiences have been invaluable lessons, not only in managing a business but also in my personal growth as a leader. They have strengthened my understanding of the importance of ethics, objectivity, and collaboration.

These learnings have shaped the way I lead LWS today, with a more open, collaborative, and strategic mindset.

Between Dreams and Reality: The Perseverance of an Entrepreneur

If I had to share one essential lesson from my journey with LWS, it would be that realizing your dreams requires hard work and unwavering perseverance. Dreaming is the starting point, but to turn those dreams into reality, action and effort are indispensable. Without ambitions or projections into the future, it is difficult to find the path to success and happiness.

An Innate Calling to Entrepreneurship

. . .

From the beginning, entrepreneurship was not just a choice for me, but rather a calling. I never questioned the possibility of doing anything else. It was as if my destiny was already written, naturally guiding me toward creating and managing my own business. This inner conviction guided me through challenges and successes, pushing me to pursue my vision despite obstacles.

Writing One's Own Destiny

This belief in my entrepreneurial destiny does not mean that the path was predetermined or easy. On the contrary, it has been a source of motivation to take the reins of my future, write my own story, and actively shape my reality. Each step of my journey with LWS has reinforced my determination to follow my passion and realize my aspirations.

THE REBIRTH AND RENEWAL OF LWS.FR

*A*round 2008-2009, I made the significant decision to focus our efforts on the LWS.FR brand, setting aside sub-brands such as A-a-hebergement, Mister-Hosting, and Hebergeur-Discount.com, which were nevertheless prosperous at the time. Why this change of direction? In retrospect, I believe it corresponded to a desire to symbolize the rebirth of LWS: a period marked by our transition to the server rooms of Sivit, our switch to Linux, and our first experiments with virtualization.

CREATING THE **LWS.FR** WEBSITE: **A Personal and Collaborative Effort**

The creation of the LWS.FR site was partly a personal project. At that time, I was still actively involved in the web development of the company. However, the design was not my doing. A designer friend, whom I had met at school, brought his expertise to design the aesthetics of this first site. Although LWS.FR already existed before, it was neither optimized for sales nor truly representative of our new direction.

LWS.FR: A Symbol of Transformation and Innovation

This refocus on LWS.FR was more than just a marketing decision. It represented a key step in the company's history, symbolizing our willingness to innovate and reinvent ourselves. This site embodied our commitment to offer more efficient services tailored to the evolving needs of our clients. It was the beginning of a new era for LWS, marked by continuous growth and increased recognition in the web hosting market.

Sidebar: From Web Integration to Business Management

Throughout the early years of LWS, I always enjoyed integrating and developing the websites myself. This passion for web creation was driven by the speed and control I had acquired, especially with HTML tables, a tool I loved to use. At that time, developing a complete website was a quick process for me, often quicker than using modern tools like WordPress, which can sometimes become real puzzles, despite their popularity.

The Decision to Focus on Management

However, over time, I realized that my primary role was to lead and manage the company, rather than getting directly involved in web development. This realization marked a turning point in my career. Although I was capable of creating a site quickly and efficiently, it became clear that my time and skills would be better utilized by focusing on the overall strategy and growth of LWS.

The Evolution of Web Technology and Its Impacts

This evolution coincided with changes in web technology. While sites were once built with HTML tables, the era of WordPress and modern CMS brought a new dimension, often more complex and time-consuming. Despite this, I kept a close eye on technological trends, ensuring that LWS remained at the forefront of innovation while delegating technical creation to expert hands

WordPress: Initially a Critical View

When WordPress appeared on the web development scene, my reaction was one of skepticism. Having started in web development about a decade earlier, I perceived WordPress and Joomla as tools for those who didn't have deep technical skills in PHP, CSS, or MySQL. To me, they were amateurs' playthings, simplified solutions to create websites without being true developers. WordPress, in particular, was initially categorized as a blogging platform, which reinforced my impression that it was more of a gadget than a serious tool.

WordPress and the Era of Forums

At the time of WordPress's emergence, forums were very popular; they were the main places for online exchange and sharing, long before social networks like Facebook came along. In this context, the idea of creating a blog seemed superfluous to me. Why maintain a blog to tell your life story when forums already provided a space for discussion and sharing?

My Initial Perception of WordPress

I must admit that I greatly underestimated WordPress. At the beginning of LWS, I had a clear-cut view: WordPress didn't bring anything new, just a combination of PHP and MySQL, and thus didn't particularly interest me.

I felt it wasn't for true tech enthusiasts like myself. Nonetheless, I was willing to host WordPress sites to meet market demand, even though I didn't yet see its full potential.

Becoming a Registrar: A Crucial Step for LWS

LWS's decision to become a domain name registrar was a major and complex strategic choice in 2013. I would especially like to thank a collaborator who supported and motivated this initiative from the start. Becoming a registrar is not just a technical matter; it's a long-term commitment that involves complex legislative and operational aspects.

In reality, it all started in 2009, with the AFNIC accreditation for .fr, followed by .be, .lu, and .eu in 2012. The big challenge came in 2013 with obtaining ICANN and Verisign accreditations for .com domains.

The Responsibility of a Registrar

As a registrar, our role is to officially register domain names for our clients, making them accessible on the Internet. This may seem simple in theory, but domain name management is a complex operation, especially given their crucial importance in today's digital world. Despite their seemingly low cost - a few euros per year - the backstage management is much more significant.

Domain Names: More Than Just a Rental

Many web hosts, even larger than LWS, are just domain resellers. However, being a registrar offers a guarantee of responsibility and direct service to the end customer. I strongly advise against buying domains through resellers. A domain name is actually an asset that is rented periodically, usually every year. No one truly owns it - we are rather tenants with benefits.

Priority and Regulation of Domain Names

It is important to highlight that owning a registered trademark does not automatically confer priority for acquiring a corresponding domain name. The .com domains have often been allocated on a 'first come, first served' basis, while the .fr domains have been subject to more nuanced regulation.

In short, the domain name field is a complex and fascinating world where LWS has made its mark as a responsible and innovative player.

LWS: A Major Player in Domain Names in France

LWS has established itself as a major player in the domain name market in France, not only through our status as a registrar but also thanks to our unique philosophy when it comes to customer service. Explaining all aspects of domain names in detail would be a daunting task, but it is essential to highlight our distinctive approach.

Details of Services Included with LWS Domain Names

At LWS, every domain name purchased comes with a set of essential complementary services, designed to enrich the user experience and provide immediate added value. These included services are:

1. **Email Addresses**: We offer the ability to create personalized email addresses, allowing our clients to benefit from professional and consistent communication with their domain.
2. **Small Web Hosting of 2 GB**: To accompany the domain name, we provide 2GB of web hosting space. This space is ideal for hosting an initial

website or a landing page, giving clients a strong starting point for their online presence.

3. **Ability to Create 3 Web Pages with a Site Template-Based Software**: We provide a user-friendly tool to create up to three web pages. This software, based on pre-designed templates, allows for quick and professional online publishing, even for those with no prior web development experience.

An Ethic of Transparency and Complete Service

Our goal is not to compel our clients to purchase additional services after buying a domain name. We believe in a transparent, customer-oriented policy, where purchasing a domain from LWS means having access to a complete set of features for immediate and optimal use. This approach is a testament to our commitment to offering not only quality products but also exceptional customer service.

A Crucial Realization About Customer Needs

Around 2019, while LWS was doing well, I realized that I had neglected a fundamental aspect of business: listening to and precisely meeting customer needs.

I was so absorbed in the technical aspects and the reliability of services that I had forgotten the basics of trade. The principle is simple: understand the customers' needs, provide an appropriate solution, and in return, be compensated. No need for a business degree to grasp this logic.

WordPress: The Unavoidable Need of Customers

It was at this time that I had a revelation: the dominant need of customers was not just to create a website, but specifically to create a WordPress site. It wasn't a minority, but a crushing majority of our clients, about 80%, who were looking to use WordPress for their web projects. This reality hit me squarely: I had underestimated the importance of this customer need, thinking it concerned only a small part of the market.

Adjusting Strategy According to Market Needs

This realization was a turning point for LWS. It was not enough that customers were generally satisfied; it was necessary to understand and respond precisely to their dominant needs. The team told me that customers were satisfied, but this did not fully answer the crucial question: what was their main need? Recognizing that creating WordPress sites was a priority for a large part of our clientele marked a strategic shift in our commercial approach and in the offering of our services.

WordPress at LWS, a Progressive Evolution

HEADING into the years 2019 and 2020, the WordPress offering at LWS was still relatively basic. It was primarily limited to an auto-installer for a quick and easy one-click WordPress setup. At that time, we had not implemented specific marketing strategies for WordPress, nor were we actively participating in the WordPress community, such as WordCamps or other events. Our presence in the WordPress.org ecosystem was also non-existent.

THE SURGE in Demand for WordPress with Covid-19

. . .

However, around 2020, the situation began to change dramatically. With the Covid-19 pandemic, the demand for WordPress skyrocketed. Businesses and individuals, seeking to strengthen their online presence due to restrictions and lockdowns, turned to WordPress en masse. This sudden surge in demand highlighted the growing need for more sophisticated and customized WordPress solutions, beyond just one-click installation.

WordPress: An Essential Tool in Times of Crisis

This period highlighted the crucial role of WordPress as a tool for businesses and individuals to quickly adapt to an ever-changing environment. The pandemic accelerated the digital transition and made WordPress an indispensable solution for many. At LWS, this realization marked a point of reflection on the importance of further developing our WordPress offering to meet the changing needs of our clients in a post-Covid world.

Managing LWS During the Covid-19 Pandemic: Adaptation and Success

The Covid-19 pandemic was a catalyst for evolution at LWS, both in our approach to work and in our response to customer needs. Remote work, adopted due to health restrictions, brought about a new mode of operation. Personally, I found this period of confinement to be incredibly productive. Working from home allowed me to focus intensely on various projects, advancing more quickly than at the office and using work as a means to escape the anxious realities of the pandemic.

Remote Work: A Solution, but Not an End in Itself

However, full-time remote work is not an ideal solution for me. I felt a compelling need to return to the office, to regain direct social interaction with my team, and to establish a more traditional balance between professional and personal life.

These face-to-face interactions are essential for me, both for personal well-being and for team dynamics.

Thanks to the Team

I would like to express my deep gratitude to my entire team, who showed remarkable resilience and adaptability during this challenging period. Their unwavering commitment allowed LWS not only to survive this tumultuous period but also to thrive, responding effectively to the increased demand.

POST-COVID: A NEW CHAPTER

The post-Covid-19 era has opened a new chapter for us. The period has been rich in lessons and adaptations, preparing LWS to meet new challenges and seize opportunities in an ever-changing world.

A New Era for LWS Post-Covid

The post-Covid era marked a major turning point for LWS, similar to what many companies experienced. This period was synonymous with change, not only in terms of internal management but also in terms of the external perception of the company.

Growing Interest from Investors

Shortly after the pandemic, we noticed an increased interest from investors in LWS. The proposals we received far exceeded my initial expectations, revealing a surprising and flattering valuation of the company. The process of valuing a company, with its complexities and particularities, was an area I had not deeply invested myself in before. My personal relationship with the value of money and the financial aspect of the business has always been somewhat distant.

A Distracted View of Investment Offers

Faced with these investment offers, my reaction was rather detached. I skimmed through them, without really dwelling on their credibility or seriousness. At that time, my mind was not geared towards selling or partnering with investors. My focus remained on the continuous growth and development of LWS, in line with the values and goals I had set since the company's creation.

Realization and Reaction to the WordPress Error

The year 2021 was characterized by a strong persistent demand, leading me to finally recognize the importance of WordPress in the web development landscape. This realization was a key moment: it's never too late to learn and improve. I decided that LWS needed to offer better integration and support for WordPress, going beyond just providing an auto-installer.

The Impact of Personal Life on Professional Life

During the Covid period, we also observed an increase in separations and divorces, a phenomenon having a direct impact on the well-being and professional performance of our collaborators. This situation made me realize the crucial human dimension within the company, even in a technical sector such as IT.

Change in Management Style

Faced with these personal challenges encountered by my team, I adapted my management style. I realized that a company, beyond its technological and commercial dimension, is above all a human adventure. Support and understanding of each individual's personal circumstances have become even more important aspects of my management, reflecting a more humane and empathetic approach to leadership.

Family Recruitment and a Shared Vision

In 2021, facing the need to increase our staff to implement the improvements envisioned during Covid, I made a unique but significant recruitment choice: I integrated my wife into the LWS team. She knew me well before the company was created and has always been a pillar in my personal life. I will not go into the details of our private life, but one thing is certain: success in creating and managing a company greatly depends on the support of loved ones.

The Key Role of My Wife in LWS

My wife joined the LWS adventure by taking on several roles. First, she helps me organize and follow up on projects, bringing a fresh perspective and effective organization. Second, she plays an active role in developing partnerships, an important facet of our expansion strategy. Lastly, she also supports me in managing the group that owns LWS and other companies.

WHY DO WE DO WHAT WE DO?

To last in a business, it's not enough just to love what you do; you must understand why you do it. For LWS, our mission is clearly defined by our slogan: "Making web hosting accessible to all." This mission excites and motivates me. Over the past 24 years, this sector has undergone significant professionalization and evolution, allowing me to constantly take on new challenges and provide a quality service that is a staple in the French technological landscape.

SIDENOTE: Luck, Opportunity, and Self-Confidence
Many of my close ones often tell me that I was lucky to achieve the current level of success with LWS. In part, they are right, but I want to emphasize that this "luck" was largely created by myself. As I explain in this book, the success of LWS is not without its nuances. We are not the market leader,

but we still exist, we are thriving, and I still enjoy running this ethical business as much as ever.

The Hard Work Behind Success

This Saturday morning, like every day, I'm up at 6 AM, working 7 days a week. This rhythm is not a constraint but a reality of the entrepreneurial life. It's important to understand that the path to success is not easy.

This book is not a story of effortless success. There is indeed a part of luck, but above all, a lot of work and personal introspection.

Personal Evolution and Self-Confidence

I have had to evolve considerably since I was 17 years old. Sometimes I amaze myself, wondering how I managed to accomplish certain things. Humans have an incredible capacity to exceed expectations. At 17, nobody believed in me, and I could have started to doubt myself after hearing it so often. But the conclusion I draw from this experience is that you should never doubt yourself. Self-confidence is fundamental, and you must work tirelessly to strengthen it. It's a constant effort, but absolutely essential.

The Importance of Appearance and Elocution in the Business World

In the business world, especially when you aspire to manage a large-scale company, certain aspects, often overlooked, take on critical importance. Among these, appearance and oral eloquence play a major role. These skills, which may seem superficial at first glance, are actually essential for establishing credibility, authority, and trust. They are learned over time and experience, and I have made it a point to develop them throughout my entrepreneurial journey.

The Language Barrier: A Handicap in the Globalized World

Another crucial aspect in an international career is language proficiency, especially English. This is an area where I recognized my shortcomings. Neglecting language skills, particularly in a globalized professional environment, can prove to be a serious handicap. It's a lesson I learned late and at a high cost. It is now part of my personal goals to improve.

Passing on Learned Lessons to Future Generations

This realization leads me to stress to my children the importance of these skills. If I could give them one piece of advice, it would be never to underestimate the importance of appearance, elocution, and especially the mastery of foreign languages. In an increasingly connected world, these skills are not just assets; they are essential for professional success and fulfillment.

Reinvigorating LWS in a Highly Competitive Sector

In 2022, facing an ever more competitive web hosting market, LWS took decisive measures to strengthen and adapt. With the addition of new collaborators, internal reorganization, and extensive technical work, we were able to refine our understanding of customer demands. This evolution allowed us to specifically focus on improving our WordPress offering.

Innovation Around WordPress

We started by revising our auto-installer, a tool that facilitates the one-click installation of WordPress. But we didn't stop there. We launched our first WP Manager, a tool designed for simplified management of WordPress, and developed several specific WordPress plugins. These innovations marked a significant step in expanding our offering.

Introduction of Advanced Caching Systems

Another big step was the introduction of advanced caching systems, with the implementation of Varnish and Nginx on our web servers. These technologies significantly improved the speed and performance of WordPress, as well as other applications like Prestashop, Joomla, and Drupal. I personally tested these improvements to ensure their effectiveness. The verdict was clear: without these systems, the performance was significantly lower. Previously, I may have underestimated the importance of these technical aspects, but these changes proved their value.

A New Dynamic and Stimulating Competition

These initiatives have injected a new dynamic into LWS, placing us in a more competitive position. I love competition, and personally ensuring the quality and performance of our services was essential. This period was a reminder that in the world of web hosting, innovation and listening to customer needs are key to staying ahead in the race.

Innovating on PHP and MySQL: A Technical and Exciting Challenge

At LWS, we have made significant efforts to optimize our PHP and MySQL services, both at the hardware and software levels. The task of making a website fast and efficient today is complex and demanding, far from the simplicity of the 2000s. In this quest for efficiency, we have integrated advanced caching technologies like Redis and Memcached. These technical solutions may seem daunting to the uninitiated, but they excite me. The precision and expertise required to optimize the operation of a website are stimulating challenges.

Exchanges and Collaboration at the Heart of Innovation

I thoroughly enjoy discussions with my team on these technical topics. Working together to find and implement innovative solutions is one of the most rewarding aspects of my job. It is in this collaboration that the creativity and ingenuity necessary to stay at the forefront of technology lie.

Making Technology Accessible to All

My primary role, after testing and understanding these technologies in-depth, is to make them accessible to our clients, regardless of their technical knowledge level. It is essential for me that our users can fully benefit from our services without having to worry about the underlying complexities. This approach aligns with our mission to make web hosting accessible to all, simplifying technology so that everyone can take advantage of its benefits without barriers.

Towards a Thorough Mastery of WordPress and the Overall Optimization of Services

In 2023, LWS is focused on perfecting our WordPress services while continuing to optimize our other offerings. Our goal is to push WordPress innovations even further, to offer users a more intuitive, faster, and more secure experience.

Deepening Advancements on WordPress

We are working to refine every aspect of our WordPress offering, focusing on improvements such as loading speed, security, and ease of use. Our ambition is to make WordPress not only more performant but also more accessible for our clients, whether they are beginners or experts. Customer feedback plays a crucial role in this process, guiding us towards the most impactful improvements.

Optimization of Other LWS Services

Simultaneously, we continue to optimize our other services. Whether in terms of performance, security, or ease of use, each service we offer is thoroughly examined. From shared hosting to cloud solutions, dedicated servers, and email solutions, our goal is to ensure impeccable quality and reliability.

An Ongoing Commitment to Innovation

This year marks a renewed commitment to innovation and excellence. At LWS, we are convinced that the constant refinement of our services is the key to staying competitive in a rapidly evolving market. Our passion for technology and our commitment to our customers remain the driving forces behind our constant quest for improvement.

2023: The Year of Listening and Innovation at LWS

In 2023, my priority at LWS is to deeply understand our clients' needs. To achieve this, I spend a large part of my time testing and experimenting with different technologies. Our goal is to provide innovative and practical solutions to our users.

Innovations and WordPress Extensions

We have launched several WordPress plugins designed to simplify our clients' lives. We have also worked to improve our WP Manager, making it particularly suitable for web agencies.

In parallel, we introduced a PrestaShop Manager, bringing similar added value for PrestaShop users.

Innovative Tools for SEO and Flexibility

With the IPXchange tool, we offer the possibility to change the IP of a website or move it to another country, with a choice of dozens of available IPv4 addresses. This tool proves very useful for SEO. We have also integrated LiteSpeed, another web server, to meet the specific needs of some clients.

Diversity of Control Panels: Plesk, cPanel, and LWS PANEL

We have maintained our Windows hosting offer with Plesk, acknowledging the persistent demand for this solution. In parallel, we have expanded our range with hosting offers that include cPanel, in addition to our own LWS PANEL. Offering cPanel, the world's number one web control panel, was a strategic decision to better understand our customers' preferences and not to neglect a significant part of the market.

Meeting Diverse Needs

These initiatives are a testament to our commitment to providing diversified and high-quality solutions. At LWS, we are constantly seeking ways to better serve our customers by listening to their needs and responding in an innovative and effective manner.

Aside on cPanel: The Monopoly and Its Consequences

In the web hosting world, a major transformation has occurred in recent years, not only among hosting providers themselves but also in the field of management software. Today, about five groups hold 90% of the web hosting market. A similar evolution has taken place in the software sector, where cPanel and Plesk, once competitors, now belong to the same group, Webpros, forming a quasi-monopoly.

The Impact of the Acquisition on Prices

This consolidation has had significant repercussions. While it has brought technological advances, it has also led to a significant increase in costs, particularly for cPanel. Before the acquisition, cPanel adopted a per-server billing policy, with reasonable prices for VPS and dedicated servers. However, since the acquisition by Webpros, the pricing structure has changed radically. Now, cPanel charges a minimum of $40 per month for multiple accounts, plus $0.20 per cPanel account per month.

The Case of LWS: A Considerable Cost Increase

For a host like LWS, which manages thousands of accounts, this change has resulted in a considerable increase in costs. A concrete example: a park of 10 cPanel servers hosting 300 accounts each used to cost around $200-300 per month. With the new pricing, this cost is approximately $1000 per month, representing an increase of about five times the initial price. This confirms the significant advantage of maintaining and developing our own LWS Panel, a strategic decision that has allowed us to remain competitive and independent in the face of this growing market monopoly.

Annual Price Increases of Plesk and cPanel

Since their acquisition by Webpros, Plesk and cPanel have adopted a policy of annual price increases, around 3 to 5%. This increase is clearly announced on their respective websites, leaving hosting providers the choice to continue with these services or not.

Although Plesk has maintained a pricing model quite close to that before the acquisition, cPanel has made more radical changes, raising questions about the sustainability of this pricing model.

The Absence of Sophisticated Direct Competitors

Currently, cPanel and Plesk face no direct competitor offering an equivalent level of sophistication. This monopolistic situation allows them to dictate their pricing policy without fear of losing a significant market share. For hosting providers dependent on these solutions, these repeated increases represent a significant financial challenge.

The Financial Impact of Pricing Changes

A simulation on a park of 500,000 cPanel accounts highlights the considerable impact of these price increases.

Although cPanel and Plesk have undergone notable improvements, these advances have come at a price, passed on to the end-users. Hosts are thus faced with a dilemma: to absorb these additional costs or pass them on to their clients while potentially seeking more affordable alternatives.

My View on Hosting Management Panels

In my opinion, the current situation of the hosting management panel market, dominated by Plesk and cPanel, reflects a simple reality: so far, no one has developed better alternatives. The sophistication and complexity of these tools somewhat justify their high cost.

Quality Comes at a Price

As a web hosting professional, I recognize the value that these panels bring to our industry. Their ability to simplify and streamline the management of a large number of sites and hosting services is unmatched. It is a significant technical achievement that logically carries an associated cost.

A Market Awaiting Innovation

However, recognizing the quality of Plesk and cPanel does not mean that the market would not benefit from increased competition. Indeed, the entry of new players could stimulate innovation and potentially lead to lower prices while offering more diverse options to hosting providers and their clients.

The Importance of Control Panels at LWS

At LWS, as well as at other major hosting providers, we have developed our own control panels. Although they may be perceived as slightly less sophisticated than cPanel or Plesk, they effectively meet 90% of our customers' needs. Moreover, their ease of use is a major asset, especially for those who are not technical experts.

Adaptation and Flexibility: Keys to Success

Unlike the telecommunications sector, where changing phone brands is relatively simple, in web hosting, switching from one control panel to another can require a significant adaptation phase for the client. Each panel has its peculiarities and logic, which can represent a challenge for users when they change providers.

The Diversity of Options at LWS

That's why it's crucial for LWS to offer a variety of control panels. By having our own LWS PANEL, as well as cPanel and Plesk in our offering, we give our clients the freedom to choose the solution that best suits their needs and skills. This diversity is a key element of our strategy to ensure customer satisfaction and facilitate the management of their web hosting and services.

Marketing in Web Hosting: Between Influence and Reality

Marketing in the web hosting sector is a complex and often opaque game. In a hyper-competitive market, making a place for oneself or maintaining a dominant position is a significant challenge. Without going into specifics that could harm LWS, I can say that a lot in this sector relies on influence and product placement.

Influence and Product Placement: An Unavoidable Reality

Product placement, a common practice in many sectors, has become an essential marketing tool in web hosting. Hosting recommendations and rankings, often perceived as objective, are sometimes the result of sponsorships or commercial agreements. This reality raises questions about the authenticity and credibility of the information available to consumers.

Beyond Keywords: The Need for an Innovative Marketing Strategy

My conclusion is as follows: in the current era, it's no longer enough to simply buy keywords and claim to be the best host at the best price. To exist and stand out in this field, it is crucial to adopt a more nuanced and strategic marketing approach, going beyond traditional methods. This involves understanding market dynamics, intelligently exploiting channels of influence, and always looking for innovative ways to attract and retain customers.

THE POSSIBILITY OF RETRACING THE PATH OF LWS TODAY

A question that is often asked is whether it would be possible to do today what I accomplished with LWS. The answer is straightforward: starting from scratch to become a web host and make a living from it quickly is extremely difficult, if not improbable, without significant means. The web hosting market has undergone significant consolidation, and competition is now globalized.

A DEMANDING and Professionalized Market

To emerge in this sector today, it's not enough to have a good idea or a passion for technology. Communication and marketing, although more diverse than before, have also become professionalized. Achieving the visibility and credibility needed to attract customers requires significant investments, both in terms of time and financial resources.

The Particular Case of France

Regarding the French web hosting market, I am skeptical about the possibility of replicating a journey similar to mine without substantial financial and strategic support. The barriers to entry are high, and newcomers must face well-established giants. In other countries, the situation might be different, but the globalization of the market makes the task difficult everywhere in the world.

Carving Out a Path in France Against the Web Hosting Giant

When asked how I managed to position myself in France against the number one European company, very aggressive in the market, my answer is nuanced. First, it is important to recognize that this leader has a considerable lead over LWS, but it is also crucial to understand that quantity does not always equal quality. There was a huge demand in the market that he was able to seize by taking bigger risks than me and by quickly surrounding himself with a competent team.

Risks, Personal Commitment, and Passion

Starting from nothing, with little to lose, my progression has been littered with considerable risks and deep personal commitments. I had to fully invest myself in numerous projects before I could consolidate LWS. This passion for my profession and the willingness to innovate off the beaten path have been my greatest strengths.

Innovation and Risk-Taking: The Keys to Success

The number one hosting provider in Europe, also French, has managed to stand out by innovating, creating its own methods and data centers, including the use of water-cooled servers, a bold innovation at the time. He took risks that few were willing to take. I have no doubt about the enormous amount of time and energy he dedicates to maintaining his dominant position. It is proof that, in our industry, innovation and risk-taking are essential to stand out and succeed.

The Energy Crisis and Its Impact on Web Hosting

The energy crisis of 2023 has been a turning point for the web hosting industry, including LWS. Once, electricity in France was affordable, which gave a significant advantage to local data centers. But with the significant increase in energy costs, France has lost this advantage, to the point that some hotter European countries now offer more attractive deals in their data centers, a situation previously unthinkable.

Innovations in Data Centers

Data centers have innovated to face these energy challenges. Solutions such as passive cooling, using water stored in systems, cold aisles, and even immersion servers (although rare) have helped optimize energy consumption. However, in terms of air conditioning, there is not yet a revolutionary solution that is widely adopted.

LWS's Environmental Commitment

At LWS, we have always chosen environmentally responsible partners, favoring sources of sustainable electricity supply and efficient methods of server containment. The use of chilled water to store cold energy accumulated at night and the use of free cooling are among the strategies we employ to minimize our energy footprint.

Software Innovation and Energy Management at LWS

In terms of software, LWS has innovated by adopting virtualization long before it became the norm. This allowed us not to allocate a dedicated server for a single site, a very energy-consuming practice. We have long worked to provide power exactly adapted to our clients' needs, calculating the energy requirement to the exact watt and offering a flexible system to avoid any slowdown. Although I cannot disclose all the technical details, these strategies are essential and constitute a part of our success and our environmental responsibility.

Customer Support: Key to Satisfaction and Success at LWS

Customer support is, without a doubt, the lifeline in the web hosting industry. I have observed competitors grow rapidly with a strategy focused on a single product and a single control panel, often centered around WordPress. This simplified approach, although effective, carries risks, particularly dependency on a single technology. At LWS, we have chosen a different path, perhaps less opportunistic, but which seems to us more prudent and sustainable.

Diversity of Services and Complexity of Support

Our extensive range of services and control panels makes customer support at LWS more complex. Training our technicians to be competent across a variety of technologies and platforms is a significant challenge. That's why we have developed powerful internal tools, designed to quickly and efficiently solve our clients' problems.

Commitment to Service Quality

Our commitment to the quality of our customer support is reflected in our current score of 4.7 out of 5, based on thousands of verified customer reviews. While this rating is satisfactory, we do not settle for it. Our goal is to continually improve the customer experience by adapting to their needs and refining our services. The diversity of our offerings, far from being a weakness, is a strength that allows us to meet a wide range of demands and maintain a relationship of trust and satisfaction with our customers.

The Range of Hosting Services at LWS: Beyond the Website

At LWS, our range of hosting services extends well beyond traditional website hosting. We also offer VPS (Virtual Private Server), Cloud, and Private Cloud hosting solutions. These services are designed to host a variety of applications and services, not just websites.

Shared Hosting: An Evolving Offer

An interesting aspect of our offer is that our current shared hosting is almost like a mini VPS. Thanks to technological advances, even in a shared environment, our clients benefit from dedicated and isolated resources (CPU, memory, IO, space), without having root access, which simplifies management while offering optimal performance.

VPS Services: A Complete Solution

As for our VPS services, they are of a complexity and completeness that would deserve a chapter of their own. In summary, our VPS offer flexibility and power suited to a wide range of needs, from simple web applications to more complex enterprise projects. However, I choose not to expand on this subject in this book, as it is a vast and technical field.

Complex Management of Email Services and Spam at LWS

In the field of web hosting, managing email services is perhaps one of the most complex aspects, especially when it comes to fighting spam. This task involves navigating through a constantly evolving labyrinth of technical standards, such as DKIM and SPF, and facing challenges such as IP banning by other hosts or providers.

The Race for Reputation and Compliance

For LWS, optimizing this service so that our clients can

use it without worrying about the technical details has been a long and challenging journey.

Ensuring the delivery of emails to providers like Gmail, Yahoo, or Outlook without ending up in spam is a technical feat. It's not just a matter of configuration through a control panel; the reputation of IP addresses and their number plays a significant role.

The Challenges of Blacklisting and Rapid Responses

The slightest misstep can lead to the blacklisting of an entire network by providers like Orange, Free, or Gmail, impacting our clients' ability to send emails to these destinations. In such situations, every minute counts to find a solution and negotiate with these providers, who are not always responsive.

Navigating a Professional and Understanding Environment

Although everyone in this sector is generally understanding and professional, it is crucial not to abuse these relationships to avoid turning interactions into power struggles. At LWS, we have developed real expertise in managing email services, ensuring we always stay within the standards and maintain a good reputation for our IPs, which is essential to guarantee the quality and reliability of our email services.

Network Management at LWS: A Significant Challenge

Network management is a fundamental and extremely complex aspect of the web hosting field. At LWS, this task has represented a significant challenge, especially concerning the manipulation and securing of IPv4 and IPv6 protocols. The IPv4 protocol, still widely used, is inherently flawed, requiring constant patches to compensate for its shortcomings and secure its many vulnerabilities. This reality makes network management a playground for both web hosts and hackers and other malicious actors.

Learning and Security Challenges

Over the years, LWS has learned to navigate this complex environment, not without some cold sweats and significant challenges. Network security has always been an absolute priority, and critical situations have been managed with remarkable professionalism and efficiency.

Thanks to the Team and Partners

I would like to express my deepest gratitude to all LWS collaborators involved in managing our network. Their composure, expertise, and performance have been essential in maintaining the stability and security of our infrastructure. Special thanks also to our partners, whose innovations have greatly contributed to strengthening our network.

The high cost of professional network equipment, such as routers and switches, leaves no room for error. The rigorous and competent management of these resources is a testament to our team's and partners' commitment to providing reliable and secure web hosting service.

IPv6: A Major Achievement at LWS

The adoption and mastery of IPv6 at LWS is a source of considerable pride. Today, many web hosts are still slow to integrate IPv6, an often-underestimated fact. IPv6, designed to replace the aging IPv4, promises to solve many problems inherent to its predecessor. It offers an almost unlimited number of IP addresses and a communication structure that is significantly more secure and efficient.

The Challenge of Implementing IPv6

However, implementing IPv6 represents a much greater challenge than simply updating a protocol. Its complexity, both in understanding and mastering, is a major obstacle for many hosts, who often postpone this deadline. Managing both IPv4 and IPv6 simultaneously is an extremely complex task.

LWS: A Pioneer of IPv6

At LWS, we took the initiative to become "full IPv6" some time ago. All our services offered are IPv6 compatible, a significant technical achievement. This subject, both lengthy and technical, would deserve further development, especially when considering that major solutions like cPanel took time to fully adapt to IPv6.

Gratitude towards the United Teams of LWS

I would like to express my deep gratitude to all the teams at LWS for their exemplary solidarity in implementing IPv6. Their willingness to share their knowledge and skills has been a key element in our success. Adopting this technology was not a simple upgrade; it required deep understanding and flawless collaboration.

Team Spirit and Knowledge Sharing

The solidarity and knowledge sharing within our teams have allowed us to unify our strengths and together overcome the technical challenges of IPv6. This transition required exceptional teamwork, where each one contributed in their own way, sharing their expertise and learning from others.

Collective Strength for an Innovative Future

Thanks to this team spirit and solidarity, LWS has been able to not only adopt IPv6 effectively but also strengthen its positioning as a technological leader in the field of web hosting. This collective strength is the pillar of our capacity to innovate and move towards the future.

The Complexity of Security for Web Hosts

Security in the field of web hosting is a topic of extreme

complexity and crucial importance. I have chosen not to delve into the specific technical details of this issue, not only to avoid scaring off the uninitiated, but also because these aspects are often in constant evolution and highly specialized.

A High-Level Technical Challenge

Managing security for web hosts, including at LWS, involves facing sharp technical challenges on a daily basis. It encompasses a multitude of factors and risks, from protecting against external attacks to securing client data. This task requires a high level of technical expertise, constant vigilance, and a rapid ability to adapt to new threats.

A Shared Responsibility

Without getting into the frightening and complex details, it is essential to recognize that security is a top priority for any web host. It requires considerable attention and resources to ensure a safe and reliable environment. At LWS, we take this responsibility very seriously, ensuring that we offer our clients the highest possible level of security, adapted to the changing challenges and threats of the digital world. And one must never forget: the human element is also the first security flaw.

The Abuse Service at LWS: A Constant Challenge

Managing the abuse service for a web host is a real challenge, a subject that could warrant a novel in itself. At LWS, this task has become increasingly demanding and complex, especially since the 2010s. The issues we encounter are varied and often delicate, ranging from requests for site removal due to phishing, brand identity impersonation, fraudulent use of images or content, and many others.

A Growing Phenomenon and Legal Responses

What I had not anticipated when founding LWS was the

extent to which managing these abuse issues would grow. Every day brings new requests, often from lawyers, demanding quick actions that comply with the law. Regulating these issues in France is a long and complex process, not to mention the situation in other countries, where it is often anarchy.

Organization and Responsiveness: Keys to Abuse Management

Faced with these challenges, we had to organize ourselves and establish effective procedures for managing these situations. Speed and accuracy of responses are crucial because they involve not only legal and ethical issues but can also affect our reputation and that of our clients. Abuse management has become an essential part of our business, requiring constant attention and in-depth legal and technical work.

GOLBEY SILICON VALLEY !

Many people wonder how I manage to develop a technologically advanced activity while staying in Golbey. The answer is surprisingly simple. The arrival of fiber optics has revolutionized the digital world, making participating in a webinar on the other side of the world as easy as it is enjoyable. Thus, even from Golbey, it is possible to stay connected to global events and share our experiences with people all over the world.

Artificial Intelligence

It is true that once you enter our offices, we speak a different language, diving into a unique and specialized universe. This requires a curious team that shares a common passion for this sector and a pronounced attraction to innovation. In 2023, as

I write these lines, we are more than ever at the heart of a global revolution driven by artificial intelligence technology. At LWS, we have not missed this opportunity. We have already developed tools using artificial intelligence to assist our clients in managing their emails, a first in our industry.

Constant Innovation

When I come across something impressive in technology, my eyes light up with curiosity. Far from intimidating me, these discoveries stimulate my desire to understand how they work and what technologies are used to achieve them. It is this fascination with innovation that fuels my passion and desire to learn.

I constantly have the desire to discover and test new technologies and innovations that emerge in our sector, in order to find useful applications to improve our services and democratize them for our clients. It's a complex process, but once the potential benefits for the clients are realized, I fully commit myself to finding innovative solutions. Reflecting on our history with WordPress, I realize the mistake of having underestimated this software so prized by our clients. Today more than ever, I actively use it, learning in detail its features and new developments. When I spot a useful function that does not exist or could be improved, I set to work.

Technological Details

At LWS, we are now developing our own WordPress plugins, an initiative still rare among hosts to this day. We are deepening our expertise in WordPress, aiming to excel in this area. We design advanced caching systems so that sites are ultra-fast while minimizing energy resource consumption.

This requires a dive into the technical details of optimization on the server side, network, and web development to integrate into the software. For the client, it comes down to a simple click on "OPTIMIZE my site," without seeing all the backstage work and the necessary adjustments to carry out such a project. But in the end, the WordPress sites we host are among the fastest in the world, without the client having to spend considerable amounts each year for powerful web hosting and additional modules. It's these kinds of details that position us among the market leaders.

CONCLUSION: A JOURNEY OF PASSION AND COMMITMENT

In this month of November 2023, as I finalize this book, I take a moment to reflect on the journey traveled. LWS, the company I founded over 23 years ago, has been an adventure of a lifetime, marked by passion, commitment, and a constant will to innovate. Although I could not cover subjects like artificial intelligence, whose future integration at LWS fascinates me, I hope to have succeeded in conveying the essence of this incredible adventure.

A Message of Gratitude and Acknowledgment

This book is an expression of gratitude towards all our customers, those who have trusted us and accompanied us in our growth. I would also like to offer my apologies to those for whom our services did not meet their expectations, while assuring that we will continue to work tirelessly to remain competitive and offer excellent service.

A Source of Inspiration for Future Generations

I also write for my children, hoping that this story will

help them better understand the profession and industry that have so passionately engaged me. If this story can inspire a new generation of entrepreneurs, ignite their curiosity and thirst for innovation, then this book will have achieved its most noble purpose.

An invitation to join the LWS adventure

As I close this book, my motivation to continue the LWS adventure is stronger than ever. If the story of LWS has inspired you and you are passionate about the technologies shaping the future of the web, I invite you to join us. At LWS, we are always looking for enthusiastic talent to enrich our team.

Join us, no matter where you are

Don't let distance be an obstacle. Whether you are nearby or on the other side of the world, we are ready to organize a meeting or a video conference to discuss opportunities. If you are convinced, as I am, that these technologies can positively transform the web, then do not hesitate to get in touch. Come and contribute to the LWS edifice and participate in its exponential development.

THANKS

As I close this book, I want to express my deep gratitude to all those who have contributed to the story of LWS. First and foremost, I thank our loyal customers, without whom our journey would not have been possible. Your trust and support have been the engine of our success and continuous innovation.

A special thank you to the entire LWS team, whose dedication, expertise, and passion have been essential to our growth and evolution. Your hard work and commitment to excellence have shaped the company we are today.

I am also grateful to my family and friends for their unwavering support, advice, and patience throughout this demanding journey.

Finally, I would like to thank everyone who took the time to read this book. I hope that the story of our adventure has inspired you and provided insight into the passion and perseverance required to succeed in the world of web hosting and beyond.

ADDITIONAL THANKS

I would also like to express my deep gratitude to Éric S., a former entrepreneur with whom I had the privilege of working for over a year. His guidance and advice were crucial in my personal and professional progress, particularly around the year 2016, when I reached significant milestones in the development of LWS.

Éric, your experience, wisdom, and support have played an indispensable role in my growth as a business leader. You helped me navigate through complex challenges and make crucial decisions that greatly contributed to the success of LWS.

Your mentorship has been one of the pillars of my journey, and I am infinitely grateful for the positive impact you have had on my life and on that of LWS.

WEBSITE

Dive into the heart of the LWS epic through this selection of some historical snapshots, capturing moments of our adventure. Each image is a living testimony of our journey, reflecting the spirit of innovation and passion that drive us. As we continue to write our story, we share our daily life and progress on the most dynamic current platforms.

The LWS website: https://www.lws.fr/
My personal website: https://depredurand.com/
Our networks:
YouTube, https://www.youtube.com/lwshosting
Instagram, https://www.instagram.com/lws_lws.fr/
Facebook, https://www.facebook.com/lws.fr
LinkedIn, https://fr.linkedin.com/company/lws---ligne-web-services
Blog, https://blog.lws-hosting.com/
Tutorial, https://tutoriels.lws.fr/

WEBSITE

These photos, more than just a memory, are a reflection of our commitment and our evolution over time.

At the beginning

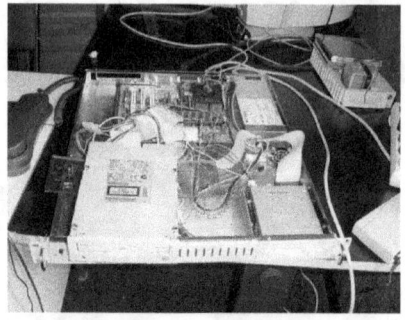

WEBSITE

WEBSITE

Today

WEBSITE

Glossary:

This glossary has been carefully designed to enrich your understanding of the technical and specialized terms used throughout this book. Hoping to have included as many relevant terms as possible, it provides clear and concise explanations to facilitate your reading and deepen your knowledge of the subject.

ADSL (Asymmetric Digital Subscriber Line): A type of high-speed internet connection that uses existing telephone lines, offering higher download speeds than upload speeds.

IP Addresses: Unique numerical identifiers assigned to each device connected to a computer network that uses the Internet Protocol, essential for communication and data exchange on the network.

AFNIC (French Association for Internet Naming in Cooperation): The French organization that manages internet domain names for France, including .fr domains. Responsible for the assignment and management of domain names, the architecture, and the stability of the French domain name system.

Apache: A widely-used open-source web server known for its robustness, flexibility, and support for various modules to enhance web functionalities

API (Application Programming Interface): A set of protocols, tools, and definitions that allow different software applications to communicate and interact, facilitating the creation and integration of software.

ASP (Active Server Pages): A server-side programming environment for creating dynamic web pages, often incorporating scripts in VBScript or JavaScript.

CentOS (Community ENTerprise Operating System): A business-oriented Linux distribution, derived from Red Hat Enterprise Linux sources, known for its stability and security.

CMS (Content Management System): A software system that facilitates the creation, management, and modification of content on a website without requiring specialized technical knowledge in web programming.

Multi-core CPU: A type of central processing unit in a computer that has multiple processing cores, allowing for better management of simultaneous tasks and increased computing performance.

CSS (Cascading Style Sheets): A style sheet language used to describe the presentation of a document written in HTML or XML, including colors, layout, and fonts, thus allowing control over the visual appearance of web pages.

Data Center: A large-scale facility housing computer equipment, such as servers and storage devices, used for processing, storing, and distributing data.

Debian: A popular Linux distribution, known for its

stability and broad array of software packages, often used as a base for other distributions.

DKIM (DomainKeys Identified Mail): An email authentication protocol that allows recipients to verify that an email was indeed sent and authorized by the domain owner, thus helping to combat phishing and spam.

DNS (Domain Name System): A system that translates Internet domain names into IP addresses, facilitating user navigation on the web.

DOS (Disk Operating System): A command-line-based operating system, most notably known as MS-DOS, widely used on personal computers in the 1980s and 1990s.

FrontPage: A former Microsoft software used for creating and managing websites, known for its user-friendliness and integration with other Microsoft products

FTP (File Transfer Protocol): A standard network protocol for transferring files between a client and a server on a computer network.

FTPS (File Transfer Protocol Secure): An extension of FTP that adds SSL or TLS security layers to encrypt the file transfer.

HTML (Hypertext Markup Language): The standard markup language for creating web pages, defining the structure and content of a web page.

HTTP (Hypertext Transfer Protocol): A communication protocol used to transmit data on the World Wide Web, often used to load web pages from a web server to a browser.

HTTPS (Hypertext Transfer Protocol Secure): A secure version of HTTP, which adds SSL/TLS encryption to secure the transmitted data.

WEBSITE

ICANN (Internet Corporation for Assigned Names and Numbers): A non-profit organization responsible for the global coordination of the Internet's unique identifier systems, including domain names, IP addresses, and protocols, ensuring the stable and secure operation of the network.

IIS (Internet Information Services): Microsoft's web server used to host websites and web applications, supporting HTTP, HTTPS, FTP, FTPS, SMTP, and NNTP protocols.

IP (Internet Protocol): A communication protocol used to route data packets from one IP address to another across computer networks.

IPs: Plural of IP, generally referring to multiple IP addresses, which are unique numerical identifiers assigned to each device connected to a computer network using the Internet Protocol.

IPv4 (Internet Protocol version 4): The most widely used version of the Internet Protocol, responsible for identifying devices on a network and their location.

IPv6 (Internet Protocol version 6): The latest version of the Internet Protocol, designed to replace IPv4, offering a significantly larger address space and improved security features.

Basic Language (Beginner's All-purpose Symbolic Instruction Code): A high-level programming language that is easy to learn, designed to be accessible to programming beginners.

Linux: An open-source operating system based on the Linux kernel, renowned for its stability, security, and flexibility, used in many environments, from servers to mobile devices.

Mail: An electronic communication system that allows the sending and receiving of messages in digital form, used for both personal and professional communications.

MySQL: An open-source relational database management system, known for its speed and reliability in managing large amounts of data.

NTFS (New Technology File System): An advanced file system used by Windows, offering features such as security, data compression, encryption, and disk quotas.

PHP (Hypertext Preprocessor): An open-source scripting language used for developing dynamic websites, embeddable into HTML and executed on the server side.

PC (Personal Computer): A personal computer designed for use by an individual, offering a wide range of applications, from games to professional tasks

Registrar: An accredited entity that provides domain name registration services on the Internet, facilitating the registration and management of domains for users and organizations.

RIPE (Réseaux IP Européens): A collaborative organization responsible for the coordination of Internet resource management policies in Europe, including IP addresses and autonomous systems.

SEO (Search Engine Optimization): A set of techniques and strategies aimed at improving the positioning and visibility of a website or web page in search engine results.

SMTP (Simple Mail Transfer Protocol): The standard protocol for sending emails over IP networks.

SSD (Solid-State Drive): A type of data storage device using flash memory, known for its superior read/write speed, reliability, and shock resistance compared to traditional hard drives.

SSL (Secure Sockets Layer): A security protocol that provides encrypted communication between a web server and a browser, ensuring the confidentiality and integrity of data exchanged on the Internet.

SPF (Sender Policy Framework): An email validation protocol that helps prevent spoofing by verifying that messages sent from a domain are authorized by the domain's administrators.

UX Design (User Experience Design): The design process focused on creating products that provide a relevant and meaningful user experience, concentrating on optimizing usability, accessibility, and the pleasure provided in the interaction with the product.

VPS (Virtual Private Server): A virtual server offering the features of a dedicated server in a shared environment, allowing for increased customization and control

www.ingramcontent.com/pod-product-compliance
Lightning Source LLC
Chambersburg PA
CBHW071519220526
45472CB00003B/1086